Nuggets of Gold

365 short thoughts to read and reflect

'Paul, a servant of Jesus Christ to ***further the faith*** *of God's elect and their knowledge of the truth...'* (Titus 1:1)

True faith should not be frozen, always furthered!

Dedicated to Sister Ruth Eddolls (1933-2020) whose passionate preaching gave me a love for God's word since I was first born again.

Introduction

The Bible is truly special. It is made up of 2 testaments, contains 66 books, was written over a span of 1600 years, across 3 continents by over 40 authors in 3 languages - yet has a unity throughout its message, namely, God's plan of salvation for the world through His Son, Jesus Christ!

However, the Bible is not only the all-time best seller which has given structure to our planet, it has the power to change each person who reads and reflects upon its words. The truth does set us free! It is likened to a 'lamp' that gives light to our path (Ps. 119:105), it is a 'hammer' that breaks the hard heart (Jer. 23:29), it is a 'sword' to defend and attack the enemies of our souls (Eph. 6:17), it is a 'mirror' that shows the real us (Jam. 1:23-24) and it is a 'seed' that is alive and kicking (1 Pet. 1:23).

God's Word! Discover it, delve into it and let your faith be developed. May these daily devotional thoughts be a source of blessing to you.

Steven Jenkins

JANUARY

1st January

'They began the consecration on the first day of the first month' (2 Chron 29:17)

When the young Hezekiah looked into the Temple on the **first** day of the **first** month of his reign, he noticed that the Temple was defiled (v5), the lamps had been put out (v7) and the offerings were not being made (v7).

On this the **first** day of the **first** month of the year, let's look into our own 'temple' and:

- Remove the rubbish and restrictions - Waste (Heb. 12:1)
- Relight the lamps - Word (Ps. 119:105)
- Reoffer a sacrifice - Worship (Heb. 13:15)

Make it a personal revolution and not a passive resolution!

2nd January

'I want to know Christ—yes, to know the power of his resurrection...' (Phil. 3:10)

There's a big difference between knowing about a person who was resurrected in the past and knowing the power of His resurrection in the present. The former is an act of the head, the latter, an awareness in the heart.

3rd January
'Then Nathan said to David, 'You are the man!'' (2 Sam. 12:7)

Often, past sins catch up with us sooner or later. However, the Lord doesn't reveal such mistakes in order to mock us, but to move us - into His perfect plan and purpose.
Where there is realisation, repentance and a return, restoration can take place. Failures don't need to be final - unless we let them!

4th January
'So in everything, do to others what you would have them do to you...' (Matt. 7:12)

Here is the 'Golden Rule'. Notice, firstly, what the Lord Jesus did not say:

'Do to others as they **have done** to you' (Past), but rather:
'Do to others as you **would have** them do to you' (Present).

What does this mean in practice? First, ask yourself the question, 'How do I wish to be treated?' With respect? With patience? With understanding? If so, start to treat others with such virtues and before long you'll find the majority of people's attitudes and actions toward you will start to alter.

Real change doesn't start with others, always ourselves.

5th January
'Pride goes before destruction...' (Prov. 16:18)

Don't let success go to your head.
Don't let failure go to your heart.

6th January
'Jesus, full of the Holy Spirit, was led by the Spirit into the wilderness..' (Lk. 4:1)
'Jesus returned to Galilee in the power of the Spirit...' (Lk. 4:14)

If the Lord leads you into the tunnel of testing, He is also the light to lead you out the other end - stronger than you were before.

7th January

"What do you want me to do for you?' Jesus asked him. The blind man said, 'Rabbi, I want to see." (Mk 10:51)

When asked what he wanted at that time, Bartimaeus could have given the usual pat-answer, 'Money!' However, Jesus was no ordinary passer-by so he was audacious enough to ask for a 'Miracle!' Finance would have satisfied him for a day, his faith enabled him to be satisfied for a lifetime. Now, because his sight was restored, other more superficial needs would soon be met. Think carefully about what you ask for. The Lord is aware of the circumferential problems, but more concerned about the core issues. When the latter are solved, the former usually fall into place.

8th January

'Simon Peter answered, 'Master, we have worked hard all night and caught nothing. But because you say so, I will let down the nets." (Lk. 5:5)

Success in life and ministry is not always about working harder, but working smarter. It has little to do with extra effort but everything to do with instant obedience when the Lord says 'row and throw'. God knows where, and more importantly when, we should cast and concentrate our efforts in certain waters. Working before waiting for clear instruction produces disappointment. Waiting then working usually sees full nets!

9th January

DON'T JUST STEP IN, STEP UP!

'The lot fell on Matthias who was chosen to replace Judas...' (Acts 1:26)

It would be very easy for Matthias to feel like a misfit, he was chosen during that 10 day waiting period after Jesus' ascension and before the descent of the Spirit. To the watching world he was chosen by lot or 'luck' and even Dr Luke mentions him only briefly. However, although Scripture says little about him, Church history says much - we are told he crossed not only countries but continents for the cause of Christ. He ministered effectively in Judea, then in modern-day Georgia and ended up in Ethiopia - amongst a cannibalistic tribe, eventually dying a martyr's death about AD80.

Matthias not only stepped **in** to substitute Judas but he stepped **up** to serve Jesus - and touch nations. When we find our true place in God, we are never a misfit chosen by chance but a perfect fit chosen by Christ. We're here by faith not by fate!

10th January

'He came to a broom bush, sat down under it and prayed that he might die. 'I have had enough!'' (1 Kings 19:4)

James reassuringly tells us that 'Elijah was human, just like us'. He knew successful confrontation on Mount Carmel and then a stressful crisis under a bush. Victory in one moment and then a victim of someone's threatening words the next. How easy in life to feel that we have gone from chapter 18 to chapter 19 overnight. In the former, Elijah's life had hit utopia, in the latter his life felt over. Leaving behind his companion and being in sole isolation certainly didn't help (19:3) But what was the solution? How did this ordinary man of God cope and come through? Some very practical things initially - food and drink (19:6) and plenty of rest (19:5). Later he became focussed and productive - he received a personal repurposing and commissioning to release others into ministry (19:15f). Furthermore, Elijah needed team (19:15f). Letting and keeping others in our lives is vital. No man is an island, even if we feel in isolation. Your present crisis will come to an end. Though you feel you can't survive you will, indeed, thrive!

11th January

'He saw the cloth that had been around His head, not lying with the linen cloths, but folded together in a place by itself.' (Jn 20:7)

At the dinner table in some Middle Eastern cultures when the servant sets the dinner table for the master, he makes sure that it is exactly the way the master wants it. The table is furnished perfectly, and then the servant waits, just out of sight, until the master has finished eating, and the servant would not dare touch that table, until the master was finished. Now, if the master was finished eating, he would rise from the table, wipe his fingers, his mouth, and clean his beard, and would pick up that napkin and toss it onto the table. The servant would then know to clear the table as the wadded napkin meant, 'I'm finished!' But if the master got up from the table, and folded his napkin, and laid it beside his plate, the servant would not dare touch the table, because the folded napkin meant, 'I'm coming back!'

The writer of the Fourth Gospel takes care to record that the cloth around Jesus' head was 'folded' in the empty tomb. The resurrected Christ is not finished, He's coming back!

12th January

SILENT SATURDAY

There is some debate in the Christian world regarding the activity of Jesus between Good Friday and Easter Sunday - on what is called Holy Saturday. Roman Catholic, Eastern Orthodox and most mainline Protestant churches teach that Jesus descended to a 'holding place', to Abraham's Side or Paradise on Holy Saturday to release righteous souls, such as the Hebrew patriarchs, who died before his crucifixion. Others may argue that Christ descended into Hell itself after his death on the cross to preach to the spirits held captive.

Whatever Jesus did or didn't do behind the scenes on this holy day will continue to be debated until his return. However, for his disciples who were left on earth at the time, it was a difficult day of waiting and wondering. A time to be silent and try to make sense of the previous few days. For the principalities and powers of darkness, Holy Saturday was a day of celebration and cheer - for the Roman soldiers, just another day at the 'office'.

Metaphorically speaking, 'Holy Saturdays' in our lives today can be difficult. Such 'Saturdays' are silent where we feel in spiritual limbo between the promise given by God and the final fulfilment of such a promise. 'Holy Saturdays' often lay between 'Fridays' of frenzied activity and 'Sundays' of visible fruit. They are quiet days when nothing can be seen, though something is always taking place beneath the soil. 'Holy Saturdays' in our lives are waiting times which often turn into doubting times because things are not working out as quickly and in the way we think they should.

Has God given you a promise - yet nothing? Have you prayed earnestly according to his will and word - yet no visible breakthrough? Take heart! The pain of Good Friday is always followed by the power of Easter Sunday in the economy of God. However, a day of patience has to come in between in order to foster faith.

Waiting times are not wasted times! The world will say, 'Seeing is believing', the word will say, 'Believing is seeing!'

13th January

'You will keep in perfect peace those whose minds are steadfast, because they trust in you.' (Is. 26:3)

God's people were able to sing and state these words, despite the fact they would soon be taken into captivity in a foreign land. The peace that Christ offers today is not devoid of difficulties but despite difficulties. It is never a life without storms, but finding a place of tranquility in the middle of the storm. We have never been promised a 'rose garden' existence where we are miraculously prevented from pain and problems. Rather, rose bushes have thorns and we are assured peace to persevere through the pain and problems. It was in the midst of personal, family tragedy that Horatio Spafford could pen the ageless hymn, 'When Peace Like a River'.

Today, whatever your 'lot', may your soul be well and may you experience the true 'eye of the storm' - calm within the calamity.

14th January

'After that, he poured water into a basin and began to wash his disciples feet...' (Jn 13:5)

It's easy to wash each other's feet, until you get to Judas - that's when grace has to take over! True service to others will always involve sacrifice as it involves touching the 'Judas betrayer' as well as the 'John the beloved' around us. Today, choose to take up the towel not only amongst your friends but especially your enemies. Remember, Jesus made the ultimate sacrifice of service – for both.

15th January

In Luke 5:10, Simon Peter was **called** to service after a miraculous catch of fish.
In John 21:15, he was **restored** to service after a miraculous catch of fish.
Messed up? Realise, repent, return and be restored! There is always a second, 'Follow me!' Confession to Christ, then commission by Christ.

16th January

'I call as my heart grows faint; lead me to the rock that is higher than I.' (Ps. 61:2)

Feel overwhelmed from what's around? Look to the One who is

above!

17th January

'In all your ways submit to him, and he will direct your paths.' (Prov. 3:6)

Is God your 'spare tyre' or your 'steering wheel?' He not only wants to get you out of the difficulties of life, He wants to guide you into His destiny for your life.

18th January

'Those who have worked only one hour have received the same payment as those of us who have worked all day...' (Matt. 20:12)

How easy it is to look across the 'vineyard' at others who seem to have done less in God's kingdom yet are receiving the same, if not more, blessing than others that have faithfully served the Master for much longer. God's economy of grace rarely makes sense or adds up. Though God sometimes seems 'unfair' true grace is never 'fair'. At the end of the day, be thankful that we serve the One who shows not only grace but mercy - He doesn't treat us 'as our sins deserve' (Ps. 103:10).

19th January

'Whatever your hand finds to do, do it with all your might...' (Eccl. 9:10)

The razor blade is sharp but can't cut down a tree,; the axe is strong but can't cut someone's hair. Everyone is important according to their own unique purpose given by the Creator. Never look down on anyone unless you are admiring their shoes

20th January

'See, your king comes to you, gentle and riding on a donkey.' (Matt. 21:5)

'Now I saw heaven opened, and behold, a white horse. And He who

sat on him was called Faithful and True..' (Rev. 19:11)

At Christ's first coming He rode in on a donkey - a symbol of **peace.**
At His second coming He'll ride in on a horse - a symbol of **power.**

Are you ready? He said, 'I will send my Spirit' and He has. He said, 'I will build my Church' and He is. He said, 'I will come again'... and He will. He'll come for those who wait (1 Cor. 1:7), for those who watch (Matt. 24:42) and for those who witness (Matt. 24:14).

21st January

'Then Jesus was led by the Spirit into the wilderness to be tempted by the devil.' (Matt. 4:1)

It's incredible to see the contrast in Scripture - to go from the 'mountain top' to the 'valley' so very quickly. In the previous chapter, Matthew 3, we read of Jesus identifying with us by public baptism, now he is identifying with us through private temptation:

- Then the cool waters of the Jordan; now the hot barren wilderness.
- Then the huge crowds; now solitude and silence.
- Then the Spirit rests like a dove; now the Spirit drives Him into the wilderness.
- Then the public voice of the Father calling Him "Beloved Son"; now the private hiss of Satan the tempter.
- Then anointed; now attacked.
- Then the water of baptism; now the fire of temptation.
- First the heavens opened; now hell closes in.

The contrast of Matthew 3 and Matthew 4 are extreme but Jesus conducted himself impeccably through both experiences. How will we respond to the 'chapter changes' in our lives?

22nd January

PRODUCTIVITY IN ISOLATION

'John...was on the island of Patmos....On the Lord's Day I was in the Spirit, and I heard behind me a loud voice...' (Rev. 1:9-10)

Often the Lord draws us to lonely places, away from distractions and daily routines, so that we can discern and discover His ways and will for both the present and the future – for ourselves and for others.

A waiting time doesn't need to be a wasted time.

23rd January

'Tongues, then, are a sign for the unbeliever....if an enquirer comes in while everyone is prophesying they are convicted and the secrets of their hearts are laid bare. They will fall down and worship God, exclaiming, 'God is really among you!" (1 Cor. 14:22, 24-25)

In our striving for 'attractional Church' amongst millennials and post-post-moderns, the tendency is to choreograph our meetings within an inch of their lives! Our desire to be 'seeker sensitive' to the outsider often verges on what we think the enquirer wants, instead of what the Spirit wants. It's often a matter of what makes us uncomfortable in the presence of the unchurched rather than what actually makes them feel uncomfortable. One of the first things omitted from the 'run sheet' are the gifts of the Spirit, especially tongues, sometimes prophecy. Our Pentecostal churches tend to be Pentecostal by name only, not by nature.

However, the Apostle Paul would disagree. When writing to the Corinthian Church, there was clearly an important place for such gifts whilst the unbeliever was present in the meeting of God's people. In addition, it was recognised tongues on the Day of Pentecost that got the attention of at least 3000 Jews - power and then preaching led to their conversion.

Spiritual gifts, when used appropriately and with explanation are surely the greatest form of 'attractional Church.' There are somethings that the 'run sheet' must make room for.

24th January

'Peter replied, 'Repent and be baptized, every one of you, in the name of Jesus Christ for the forgiveness of your sins...'' (Acts 2:38)

The Scriptures do not teach 'penance' but 'repentance'. The former seeks to 'right a wrong' until the next time, whereas the latter is a complete turning away from wrong - full stop! A fundamental difference exists between the two.

25th January

'Paul and his companions travelled throughout the region of Phrygia and Galatia, having been kept by the Holy Spirit from preaching the word in the province of Asia.' (Acts 16:6)

'As was his custom, Paul went into the synagogue and reasoned with them from the Scriptures.' (Acts 17:2)

In mission, being aided by God's Spirit and adopting a good strategy are not opposed to each other. Like both blades on a pair of scissors they work together to achieve the aim. To see fruit, there needs to be a framework and faith.

26th January

'In the year that King Uzziah died, I saw the Lord, high and exalted... "Woe to me!" I cried. "I am ruined! For I am a man of unclean lips..."And I said, 'Here am I. Send me!" (Is. 6:1, 5, 8)

According to this scripture, three things can happen in the presence of the Lord. Firstly, we see how holy God is (v1). Secondly, we see how unworthy we are (v5). Thirdly, we see how a Holy God can use unworthy people (v8).

Know the power of God's sovereignty, know the forgiveness of your personal sin, then know the responsibility of purposeful service.

27th January

'When Peter saw the disciple whom Jesus loved he asked, 'Lord, what about him?' Jesus replied, 'What has that got to do with you?'' (Jn 21:21-22)

Don't compare yourself with other spiritual athletes perhaps further down the field but run your own race in the lane marked out for you. Because we tend to run towards what we look at, if we look too much at others, not only are we in grave danger of drifting off course and risking disqualification but it may produce the same sharp response that Peter received from the One waiting at the finishing line.

28th January

MINISTRY LESSONS FROM JOHN 6 (Part 1)

'When Jesus looked up and saw a great crowd coming toward him, he said to Philip, "Where shall we buy bread for these people to eat?" He asked this only to test him, for he already had in mind what he was going to do.' (Jn 6:5-6)

Ministry doesn't always come from hearing a vertical 'call' from above, but by seeing a horizontal challenge from around. With the former, you could wait forever but with the latter, you have to act now!

The need becomes the 'call'.

29th January

MINISTRY LESSONS FROM JOHN 6 (Part 2)

'Jesus then took the loaves, gave thanks, and distributed to those who were seated as much as they wanted.' (Jn 6:11)

'I am the bread of life.' (Jn 6:35)

The Lord met the physical need before He met the spiritual need.

Social initiatives and spiritual input are the two blades of a pair of scissors – together they cut through to hearts but on their own they merely crease.

Fill stomachs and feed souls! Give soap, give soup, give salvation!

30th January

MINISTRY LESSONS FROM JOHN 6 (Part 3)

'Jesus then took the loaves, gave thanks, and distributed to those who were seated as much as they wanted. He did the same with the fish.' (Jn 6:11)

On this occasion, the Lord not only prayed but He was practical. There is a time to put your hands together and reach up to Heaven, but there is a time to unclasp those same hands and reach out to your needy world.

31st January

MINISTRY LESSONS FROM JOHN 6 (Part 4)

'Here is a boy with five small barley loaves and two small fish, but how far will they go among so many?" (Jn 6:9)

It isn't always our ability that the Lord is looking for - but our availability! When we give what we have, He's still able to take a little and make it a lot!

FEBRUARY

1st February

'Some time later the brook dried up...' (1 Kings 17:7)

In the Christian life even good and godly things come to an end. Safe places of security and supply, or brooks of blessing, can dry up leaving us in a wilderness of bewilderment. At such times we can either pine for the past or look to the Lord.

For Elijah, a man just like us (James 5:17), he knew daily provision from the Kerith Ravine where the birds brought him bread and the river brought refreshment. However, when the rain stopped the ravens left and his daily supply abruptly ended. Thank God that the true source of all is never a created creature but the Creator himself! Don't look to earthly means which often change but the heavenly Maker who never changes. Though the ravens were God's instruments of the past, the Lord had already been prompting a woman to meet the prophet's needs in the present. Though your brook may have dried up, realise that the Lord is already ahead of you. A widow is waiting in the wings!

2nd February

'..there were some who escaped the edge of the sword...Some faced jeers and flogging and were killed by the sword.' (Heb. 11:34, 36-37)

These mystifying words occur in the great chapter on the 'Hall of Faith'. Some believers escaped the sword and some endured the sword. Did the latter have less faith than the former? Some today would have to say 'Yes' as suffering and sickness only come with unbelief. Try telling Job that! Try telling Paul that! Try telling the

Early Church martyrs that!

We have to be big enough as believers to simply accept the fact that some faithful and faith-filled followers of Christ severely suffer and others do not. Some sincere and committed Christians, even after much 'prophecy' and prayer, go to Heaven whereas some are miraculously delivered from death and remain on Earth.

More often than not, it isn't a matter of faith, but just the way of the Father. Whether we live or die, whether we survive the sword or succumb to it, 'we are the Lord's' (Rom. 14:8).

3rd February

'...give me only my daily bread. Not too much that I will forget you or too little that I will dishonour you.' (Prov. 30:8b-9)

May we receive enough today from the God who is more than enough!

4th February

'So if you consider me a partner, welcome him as you would welcome me.' (Philemon 17)

Forgiveness on both sides of the door! Philemon, as a Christ-follower, had been shown God's forgiveness in the past - now he was being asked to show forgiveness in the present, to someone who had wronged him. In Scripture, these two aspects of forgiveness are usually linked together - the forgiveness we are shown vertically by God and the forgiveness we are to show horizontally to others:

'Forgive us our sins as we forgive those who sin against us.' (Matt. 6:12)
'...forgiving each other, just as in Christ God forgave you.' (Eph. 4:32)

Forgiveness is personal, but forgiveness is practical. We forgive, and go on forgiving, because we've been forgiven and go on being forgiven!

5th February

'Son, give me your heart..' (Prov. 23:26)

'Above all else, guard your heart....' (Prov. 4:23)

When it comes to our heart, the best we can do is to **give** it and to **guard** it.
Give it to the right One, guard it from the wrong things!

6th February

'In all of this you greatly rejoice, though now for a little while you may have had to suffer grief in all kinds of trials.' (1 Pet. 1:6)

It is interesting to me, not only what Scripture does say but what it doesn't say. Of course, a strong argument can never be made from silence alone - but that same silence from the writers of God's word is deafening at times. Context is key! 'Peter' is writing to a persecuted people, either through the oppression of Nero or Domitian - both severe. However, nowhere does he encourage them to pray for protection from the evil and ungodly actions that surrounds and affects them. Not once does he expect them to ask for deliverance from secular persecution. Never are they exhorted to 'bind the devil'. Peter's advice is clear, **Rejoice!** - even in the midst of mayhem. The true disciple is to be joyful not because they are without trouble but despite trouble. Such joy is not superficial, hollow happiness, with its dependence on happenings, but is constant and unshakable which has a pruning effect on our souls and future glory in store.
Christians are simply not promised immunity from suffering, in whatever form that takes. To 'name' 'claim' and 'frame' such Utopia this side of heaven has more to do with wishful thinking than scriptural teaching and seeks to raise ourselves to an unrealistic level that the New Testament doesn't teach and the saints of old never experienced.
However, regarding life's present hardships, the only thing we

are promised and guaranteed is His presence. Regarding our future hope, we can expect salvation in all its fullness. These we can rightly claim.

7th February

'If anyone be in Christ they are a new creation - the old has gone...' (2 Cor. 5:17)

'The one who deceived them was thrown into the lake of sulphur...' (Rev. 20:10)

The next time the enemy reminds you of your **past** remind him of his **future**!

8th February

"You are the light of the world" (Matt. 5:14)

The Plague of Cyprian was a pandemic that afflicted the Roman Empire from about AD 249 to 262. The plague is thought to have caused widespread manpower shortages for food production and the Roman army, severely weakening the empire during the Crisis of the Third Century. Its modern name commemorates St. Cyprian, bishop of Carthage, an early Christian writer who witnessed and described the plague. The agent of the plague is highly speculative due to sparse sourcing, but suspects include smallpox, pandemic influenza and viral fever like the Ebola virus. How did the Early Church respond to what was happening at the time? Despite the most severe period of persecution of all, the Church led the way. It did not care just for its own. It did not bury its head in the sand. It did not take proof texts from Scripture. It did not shout at the devil. It served the community and not itself. It cared for the sick, it fed the hungry, it buried the dead.

For the true Church, at times of national and international crises - we can either see such problems as **opposition** from the enemy or an **opportunity** from the Almighty. We can either shrink back or step forward - we choose!

9th February

'Samson's hair grew again...' (Jud.16:22)

When you feel your strength has gone, He's the God of the 'again!'

10th February

ROOTS & SHOOTS

'At least there is hope for a tree: If it is cut down, it will sprout again, and its new shoots will not fail. Its roots may grow old in the ground and its stump die in the soil, yet at the scent of water it will bud and put forth shoots like a plant.' (Job 14:7-9)

Feel cut down and cut back? Been pruned by problems? If there are living roots, there will be lively shoots once again. Just because the roots aren't visible it doesn't mean they're not viable. If something is alive there's always hope. Drench that which is hidden and seems dead with the water of Scripture and the Spirit....and wait. The pain of Autumn and Winter are faithfully followed by the progress of Spring and Summer with new buds for all to see.

Where are you planted - in the wisdom of the Word (Ps. 1:3) or the ways of the world (Rom. 12:2)? Look after your roots, the shoots will take care of themselves.

11th February

'...singing to God with gratitude in your hearts...' (Col. 3:16)

'...speaking to one another with psalms, hymns, and songs from the Spirit...' (Eph. 5:19)

'He will rejoice over you with singing.' (Zeph. 3:17)

Sing to God and to one another because God sings over you!

12th February

'They had such a sharp disagreement that they parted com-

pany.' (Acts 15:39)

It is a fact of ministry that sometimes leaders disagree and decide to go their separate ways. Barnabas and Saul, who were friends and colleagues, did just that after the John Mark incident. Notice how God graciously went on to bless both in their individual future missionary endeavours.

As in the Council of Jerusalem there should certainly be a place for healthy discussion and debate amongst leaders of varying layers in order to reach godly decisions and for a leader's actions and attitude to sometimes be questioned by another (Gal. 2:11). When we close down such confrontation and a leader is raised above the common herd, accountability and authenticity disappear and disaster is never far away. When iron sharpens iron, sparks will inevitably fly! The vital thing is to stay within fellowship, forgive and move forward - whether on the same or separate paths.

13th February
'Do not be anxious about anything...' (Phil. 4:6)

The devil wants you to worry about what's next so you can't enjoy what's now. He has been and always will be a liar. Stop worrying! Focus your faith on the Father. Enjoy, not endure, each day He gives.

14th February
'Though I give all my goods to feed the poor, and though I give my body to the flames, but have not love, it profits me nothing.' (1 Cor. 13:3)

Remembering St Valentinus who in 269AD was martyred under Claudius II for performing Christian marriages, refusing to deny Christ and for helping the persecuted Church of his day. He was buried on the 14th February. Tradition tells us that he prayed that Judge Asterius' daughter would be healed of blindness and she was. Before his execution, he left her a note signed 'from your Valentine'.

On this Valentine's Day, remember in love the millions of Christians around the world still suffering for their faith almost 2000 years later.

15th February

'Watch your life and your doctrine closely...' (1 Tim. 4:16)

It isn't only what we **believe** but how we **behave**. Attitude and actions! The former will influence the latter.

16th February

"Is it a time for you yourselves to be living in your panelled houses, while this house remains a ruin?" (Hag. 1:4)

Those who had returned from exile to start the process of rebuilding the Temple started to move their priorities from God's house to their own houses, from the Lord's kingdom to their own. It resulted in a sharp rebuke from the prophet to re-evaluate.

Life is short - it's a mist or a vapour - and in life there are no dress rehearsals for the main event. We can spend our days doing whatever we like but when the 'coin' is spent that's it. We need to prioritise in order to spend it right. We often have trouble with priorities. Blaise Pascal stated, 'The last thing we do is to decide what to do first'. However, priorities have benefit - they give our life focus and boundaries and help us to say that important word 'No!' They make sure we don't forsake marriage for ministry, our faith for frivolities or our children for a career.

Decide today what your priorities are and keep to the plan. Don't just do good things to keep other people happy, do God things to please Him!

17th February

'I keep asking that the God of our Lord Jesus Christ, the glorious Father, may give you the Spirit of wisdom and revelation, so that you may know him better.' (Eph. 1:17)

We receive information to know our world better, we receive revelation to know God better! Information can 'puff up' but revelation can 'build up'.

18th February

'...continue to work out your salvation with fear and trembling' (Phil. 2:12)

As followers of Christ, we are never expected to work **for** our salvation (Eph. 2:8-9), but we are encouraged to work **out** our salvation. The former is a one-off, the latter is on-going. Holiness is not only positional, it is progressive - a past act of God (1 Cor. 1:2) and a present activity of ourselves (1 Pet. 1:15).

Sanctification should follow salvation!

19th February

SPIRITUAL 'SKYSCRAPERS'

'Therefore everyone who hears these words of mine and puts them into practice is like a wise man who built his house on the rock.' (Matt. 7:24)

The story of the wise and foolish builders is a classic Bible tale. There are some similarities between the two builders:

- Both built something;
- Both chose a foundation;
- Both experienced a storm.

However, there was one striking difference between the two, one built something that survived the storm, the other built something that succumbed to the storm.
The difference was not the framework nor what the house was filled with - but the foundations. Foundations are fundamental!

The deeper the foundation, the higher the building. Spiritual 'skyscrapers' are not built overnight - there are long periods of time when deep holes are made and then filled with strong material, but out of public sight. If we want to go the distance and build something of worth, we have to dig deep. This takes time and travail and very little is in public view. The 'cement' and 'steel' that are poured and put into place is perceiving and then practicing God's word - even the difficult parts. When the inevitable storms of life come, the building stands strong though it may sway.
In our visible results oriented world don't be quick to build a framework and fill the building with what is seen of men. Give priority to building firm foundations though they are largely hidden. A biblical attitude determines altitude. Depth determines height.

20th February

'Those who hope in the Lord will soar like eagles....' (Is. 40:31)

To rise higher, eagles wait to catch the wind at the correct time and then soar - they don't frantically flap!

Waiting for the promise, or it's fulfilment, should develop patience and not panic. The former produces hope for the future. The latter, hasty decisions in the present.

21st February

"Test me in this, see if I will not throw open the floodgates of heaven and pour out so much blessing that there will not be room enough to store it.' (Mal. 3:10)

Although, generally, we should not put God to the test (Deut. 6:16) the only time the Lord commands us to test Him is in regards to financial provision.
As we **bring**, He will **bless**! He wants to prove Himself your Provider!

22nd February

'But David went back and forth from Saul to tend his father's sheep at Bethlehem.' (1 Sam. 17:15

In 1 Samuel 16, the young David is anointed as future king. In the very next chapter he is found in the fields. There is something about being willing to protect a few sheep in private before being trusted to guard a whole nation in public. To successfully lead a small flock when no one is watching before guiding an entire kingdom when everyone is watching.

Faithfulness in the present will often lead to fruitfulness in the future.

23rd February

'Formerly he was useless to you, but now he has become useful both to you and to me.' (Philemon 11)

God can take the 'useless' and make them 'useful'. What happened to the runaway slave after Paul's appeal to Philemon on his behalf? Interestingly, the great martyr, Ignatius of Antioch, writing at the turn of the 2nd century, mentions a 'Bishop Onesimus of Ephesus'. If this is the same person, he went from slave to thief to runaway to convert to brother to bishop. The gospel transforms!

Don't let your history determine your destiny!

24th February

'Then Mary took some expensive perfume and poured it over Jesus' feet....and the fragrance filled the house...' (Jn 12:3)

Mary had a choice to make - she could either save this perfume for Jesus' impending burial or she could use it there and then when her Master and Friend could appreciate it - other guests too. As my mother always said, 'I don't want flowers at my funeral - it's too late to enjoy them then!'

When is the time to offer our best to Jesus? Never later but always now. If we act in the present and not wait for the future perhaps others around us will benefit from the fragrance too.

25th February

'Then he gave the bread and fish to his disciples and they fed the people.' (Matt. 14:19)

Today, the same Lord wants to work miracles in the lives of the multitude around you. The good news is that He still wants you to be part of what he has planned. However, never in a way that you get the glory. You are not designed to be the source of blessing, merely the channel.

26th February

'......but we had hoped that he was the one who was going to redeem Israel.' (Luke 24:21)

Life and ministry have many disappointments or 'I had hoped' moments. We like to dream! However, disappointments come when we expect God to work according to our understanding. It has to be the other way around. We can never be disappointed with Him when His plan becomes our hope, when His agenda becomes our desire and His will becomes our peace.

27th February

'I did not go up to Jerusalem to see those who were apostles before I was, but I went into Arabia' (Gal. 1:17)

Before his conversion, Paul lived his life by the Law originally given at Sinai in Arabia. After his Damascus Road experience he received revelation of the Gospel of Grace - a new way to live his life - in Arabia.

Sometimes the Lord has to take us back to places in the past to learn new lessons of life for the future.

28th February

'The chief cupbearer, however, did not remember Joseph; he forgot him.' (Gen. 40:23)

'But God remembered Noah...' (Gen. 8:1)

Though people often forget us, the Lord always remembers us!

MARCH

1st March

In his final sermon before his death on the 1st March 589, St David exhorted his congregation to: “Be joyful, keep the faith, and do the little things”

Still good advice over 1400 years later! In your life today:

Keep thanking the Lord (1 Thess. 5:18)
Keep trusting in the Lord (2 Tim. 4:7)
Keep travailing for the Lord (Eccl. 9:10)

Happy St David’s Day!

2nd March

‘This day the Lord will deliver you into my hands…’ (1 Sam. 17:46)

True faith doesn’t say, ‘God can do it for others’ it says, ‘God will do it for me!’ It’s relocating from the general to resting in the personal.

3rd March

'The Sovereign Lord is my strength! He makes me as surefooted as a deer, able to tread upon the heights.' (Hab. 3:19)

The prophet was greatly troubled at both the world around him and his own world. On more than one occasion he asked the same age-old question, 'Why?' However, in the midst of **chaos**, he **chose** to praise! To rejoice is surely a choice! At that moment his eyes were lifted to the source of his strength and the security of what God could make him to be - a deer.

In times of danger, the mountain deer in the Middle East has the ability to go higher, to scale unusually difficult terrain where predators dare not go, to run securely with abandonment and to stay on track.

Today, if you are in distress, go higher! If you are being attacked, go higher! If you are questioning 'Why?' - go higher! Remember you are seated with Christ in the heavenly realms. You'll find the view from the top is simply stunning!

4th March
'We speak as men who have been tested and approved by God who has trusted us with the Gospel...' (1 Thess. 2:4)

We can only be trusted by God, when we have been tested by God. Before Joseph was trusted in Pharoah's palace he was tested in the prison. Before Abraham was trusted as a 'father of many' he had to be tested as a 'father to one.' If Moses was to shepherd God's people, he had to be faithful to his own flocks. If Jesus' temptation in the wilderness teaches us anything, a life of faith can only be lived when the flesh is truly put to death.
If this was true for the 'saints' of old, why will it be any different for us today? We trust God, but does God trust us... with his Gospel?

The pathway to true biblical success is littered with struggles - such trials need to be overcome.

5th March
'Do not fear, for I am with you; do not be dismayed, for I am your God.' (Is. 41:10)

In our world of daily phobias, anxiety and worry - be aware that God, in His Word, took the time to ensure the words 'Fear not' or 'Do not be afraid' would occur some 365 times.

6th March

'Three times I pleaded with the Lord to take it away from me. But he said to me, 'My grace is sufficient for you..." (2 Cor. 12:8-9)

'And will not God bring about justice for his chosen ones, who cry out to him day and night?' (Lk. 18:7)

Sometimes we are to pray until the problem is solved - sometimes we pray persistently yet the problem persists. Both are in the sovereign care of a Sovereign God. Wisdom and discernment help us to know the difference. Prayer is never a mantra to the great unknown, but a relationship with the One who can be known. To such a Being there is no such thing as unanswered prayer - sometimes the answer is 'Yes!' sometimes 'No!' and sometimes 'Yes, but wait a while!' Whatever the answer, God's sustaining grace is available in abundance.

7th March

'...while every branch that does bear fruit he prunes so that it will be even more fruitful.' (Jn 15:2)

I know very little about gardening. I have a tendency to pull up flowers and let weeds grow! However, the experts tell me that in cultivation, the pruning of plants is vital. It does the following:

- Removes dead and diseased branches;
- Rejuvenates the plant and encourages blooming;
- Restricts and controls the size and shape of the plant.

In other words, pruning is productive. It has a purpose. When the Heavenly Gardener prunes His people it's for our greater good. Though any cutting away is excruciating on the whole and leaves us exposed, such pain has a purpose - that which is dead and useless in our lives can be removed, our spirit is rejuvenated and boundaries, or restrictions, are put into place to help us grow correctly.
The Lord punishes His enemies, but disciplines those He loves. Discipline is a vital part of true discipleship - trust Him!

8th March

Women were the last ones at the cross of Christ (Jn 19:25) and the first ones at the tomb of Christ (Jn 20:1) - such devotion! Women were the first ones entrusted with sharing the good news of the glorious resurrection, though the male disciples did not believe them (Lk. 24:10-11) - such doubters!

Happy International Women's Day!

9th March

'But he knows the way that I take; when he has tried me, I shall come out as gold.' (Job 23:10)

In ancient times, refining precious metal involved a craftsman sitting next to a hot fire with molten gold in a crucible being stirred and skimmed to remove the impurities that rose to the top.

The irritations of life allow the impurities of life to rise to the surface of our life - to become visible and vulnerable. However, the Master Craftsman is not only interested in exposure but extraction. He is close, sitting next to you to stir and skim leaving something that is prized and profitable.

Feeling the heat? Stand firm! You are in company with the Bible greats. There is always a future purpose in the present pain.

10th March

'I chose you and appointed you so that you might go and bear fruit...' (Jn 15:16)

In Bible times, the norm was for a student of the Law to choose the master – the one they wished to learn from, listen to and live with. The rabbi would then choose the cream of the crop - those who were the brightest and with the greatest potential. They certainly did not want to invest their precious time with those who may not be able to make it in the rabbinical world.

Jesus chose the Twelve and far from being 'high-flyers' of their day, rather they were 'unschooled, ordinary men' (Acts 4:13). Praise God, He still takes the weak and the foolish to confound the strong and the wise. However, He picks us in order to be productive. Not only to function but to be fruitful through the process of testing and training.

11th March

'Then he reached out his hand and took the knife to slay his son. But the angel of the Lord called out to him from heaven, 'Abraham! Abraham!" (Gen. 22:10-11)

True faith is not exercised at the bottom of the mountain when the command to obedience is given, only at the top, when the dagger is in our hand.

12th March

"See your king comes to you riding on a donkey....the crowds shouted, 'Hosanna!'" (Matt. 21:5,9)

On that first Palm Sunday, the donkey would have been foolish to think the crowds were praising him! True 'God-carriers' should never seek the glory, they merely present the One who rightly deserves it.

13th March

'Therefore comfort one another with these words.' (1 Thess. 4:18)

For the born-again believer, whose name is written in the Lamb's Book of Life through trusting, never trying, not only is there life before death, but life after death. What happens when saved loved ones depart this world? Scripture holds the answers:

- Their soul is taken to God's presence by angels (Lk. 16:22);
- They are with the Lord (2 Cor. 5:8);
- They will receive a new body (1 Cor. 15:42-44);
- They will receive rewards at the '*bema* seat' of Christ (2 Cor. 5:10);
- They will come with Jesus when he returns soon to Earth (1 Thess. 4:14-16);

- They will keep their identity forever (Luke 22:17-18);
- True believers who are left will one day be with them and the Lord for eternity (1 Thess. 4:17, Rev. 21:3).

Though we mourn, we do not do so without hope! Biblical hope is not wishful thinking, but a certainty. God says it, I believe it, that settles it!

14th March

'Immediately he received his sight and followed Jesus along the road.' (Mk 10:52)

Arguably the greatest result of a life touched by Christ is heeding and not just a healing. Discipleship is more than an initial decision.

15th March

'But they urged him strongly, "Stay with us, for it is nearly evening; the day is almost over." So he went in to stay with them.' (Lk. 24:29)

Christ won't 'gate crash' your life! He won't barge through your door! He waits for, and then accepts, your invitation to enter. The handle to our heart is on the inside.

16th March

The Book of Acts is so called because it's a book of outward actions not just an inward attitude. It's a book of what Christ did, by His Holy Spirit, through human channels. Our beliefs are foundational - but they have to act as a springboard into behaviour. Doing follows dogma! We are always saved by faith alone, but true faith never remains alone - works should soon follow, not to become a Christ-follower but because we are a Christ-follower.

17th March

According to the 'Confession of Saint Patrick', at the age of sixteen he was captured by a group of Irish pirates. They took him to Ireland where he was enslaved and held captive for six years. Patrick writes in the 'Confession' that the time he spent in captivity was critical to his spiritual development. He explains that the Lord had mercy on his youth and ignorance, and afforded him the opportunity to be forgiven his sins and convert to Christianity. Whilst in slavery, he worked as a shepherd and strengthened his relationship with God through prayer, eventually leading him to convert to Christianity. His captivity time was a constructive time!

After six years of slavery, Patrick escaped to his home in Britain and then trained for ministry in Europe. He then returned to the same Ireland that once kept him captive and after years of sacrificial service he wrote:
'Never before did they know of God except to serve idols and unclean things. But now, they have become the people of the Lord, and are called children of God.'

Happy St Patrick's Day!

18th March

'Then the Lord God formed a man from the dust of the ground and breathed into his nostrils the breath of life, and the man became a living being.' (Gen. 2:7)

'I looked, and tendons and flesh appeared on them and skin covered them, but there was no breath in them.' (Ez. 37:8)

Often, before the Lord breathes His Spirit into something, there needs to be a structure. Bones then breath! Skeleton then Spirit! Layout then life!

Build a framework first, but make sure the framework is then filled!
Strategy of man and the Spirit of God can work together.

19th March

IT IS FINISHED! (Part 1)

'Jesus said, 'It is finished!'' (Jn 19:30)

The Greek transliterated word for these last three words of Christ on the Cross is 'Tetelestai'. I understand this word was written across business documents by merchants in New Testament times to state, categorically, that a bill had been paid in full. The Cross is the payment, the Empty Tomb is the receipt proving that such a payment was accepted by a Holy God.

Jesus said, 'It is finished!' He never said, 'I am finished!' It may have been Friday, but Sunday was coming!

20th March
IT IS FINISHED! (Part 2)

'He forgave us all our sins, having cancelled the charge of our legal indebtedness, which stood against us and condemned us; he has taken it away, nailing it to the cross.' (Col. 2:14)

The Apostle Paul is referring here to a common practice at the time where criminals serving time in jail would have their crimes listed on a note that was posted at the prison where they were kept, and it correlated the crimes to the amount of punishment they were to serve. Then, at the end of their sentence, the jail keeper would stamp the paper with 'TETELESTAI', meaning 'PAID IN FULL'.

When Jesus cried out on the cross, 'It is finished!' the payment for our sin was 'PAID IN FULL!' Three days later, God issued the receipt by raising His Son to life! Price paid, transaction complete, job done.

21st March

'Going a little farther, he fell with his face to the ground and prayed, 'My Father, if it is possible, may this cup be taken from me. Yet not as I will, but as you will." (Matt. 26:36)

The real battle of Easter wasn't just Golgotha but Gethsemane when the choice was made and self-control was exercised. At the former, Christ could have called down legions of angels for his escape, at the latter, he could have chosen an easier way.

'Not my will, but yours.....' - the words on which mankind's redemption rests.
Selfless sacrifice from Him leads to salvation for us!

22nd March

'Do not conform to the pattern of this world, but be transformed....' (Rom. 12:2)

Chameleon or caterpillar? The former seeks to change to merge in with its surroundings whereas the latter seeks to change into something different altogether and stand out.
Be transformed through a spiritual mindset not conformed to mindless society! Our world is attracted by difference not duplicates.

23rd March

LEADERSHIP LESSONS (Part 1)

'When you come, bring the cloak and my scrolls, especially the parchments.' (2 Tim. 4:13)

In previous verses, the Apostle Paul talks of his imminent departure or impending death. However, one of his final wishes was for his cloak - to warm his body, and for his scrolls - to waken his mind. Paul was still reading and learning to the very end.
Leaders are readers! Leaders are learners!

24th March

LEADERSHIP LESSONS (Part 2)

'Elisha gave word to Naaman, commander of the armies of Aram...'Go wash in the Jordan" (2 Kings 5:10)

As a commander, Naaman was used to giving instructions to others, now he had to receive an instruction from another.

Leader, never be above listening! You may miss your miracle.

25th March

LEADERSHIP LESSONS (Part 3)

'Share and share alike.....whether amongst those who went to battle or those who stayed back and guarded the equipment.' (1 Sam. 30:24)

True leaders are fair and considerate of all in the army. On this occasion David made sure all equally shared the rewards of battle, whether they fought on the front line or whether they stayed at base camp.

Leader, be loyal to all, no matter what someone's position or place. You will then find loyalty is returned to you.

26th March

'The wind blows wherever it pleases...' (Jn 3:8)

The ways of the Lord are often unpredictable yet His activity is always undeniable!

27th March

'Philip answered him, "It would take more than half a year's wages to buy enough bread for each one to have a bite!"' (Jn 6:7)

When faced with a problem, Philip resorted to finding the solution with his mind. He correctly calculated how much money was needed to buy the solution, but he was still left with a problem. Of course, God has given us brains to think and as believers, a 'renewed mind' (Rom. 12:2). However, there are times when the answer isn't in our head, but in Heaven. The solution doesn't come from our mind, but through a miracle - not from our sense, but from the Spirit.

Is there a 'mountain' that needs moving or an obstacle that needs overcoming? Don't look in, but look up!

If you have a problem, don't just 'face it' - 'faith it!'

28th March

'We were delighted to share with you not only the gospel of God but our lives as well, because you had become so dear to us...' (Thess. 2:8)

Sharing the gospel is evangelism, sharing our lives is discipleship. The command of Christ to His Church was for the latter – disciples not just decisions!

29th March

'Put on the full armour of God..' (Eph. 6:11)
'Pick up the sword of the Spirit..' (Eph. 6:17)
'Pray in the Spirit on all occasions..' (Eph. 6:18)

Put on, pick up, pray in...This is how I fight my battles!

30th March

'And being in anguish, he prayed more earnestly, and his sweat was like drops of blood falling to the ground.' (Lk. 22:44)

To give any impression that Christ was somehow immune to the pressures and stress of life is utter folly and downgrades His humanity. To imply that He lived his 33 years on earth in a bubble of prevention robs both Him and us of the marvel of His incarnational birth and incarnational ministry. He was fully God and fully human - both the Creeds and Canon of Scripture declare it. He was tempted, yet without sin. He suffered but stayed strong. He felt unimaginable pain, but didn't succumb to the devices of the enemy. He wasn't immune from life - He was involved in life!

During times of national difficulty in society, the Church has a rare chance to be a prophetic voice to our world - not only through our words but especially our works. It's an opportunity to be truly incarnational in the community - what they are going through we are going through. The only difference is that we have hope instead of helplessness, faith instead of fear and peace instead of panic. Such things never run out on God's 'shelves'.

Church - we can either shrink back or step forward. We can either claim to be immune or we can be involved. If not us, who? If not now, when? We are to be the people of God, with all that goes with it – not only in the Church building, but especially in our community.

31st March

'Near the cross of Jesus stood his mother.....When Jesus saw her there, and the disciple whom he loved standing nearby, he said to her, "Woman, here is your son," and to the disciple, "Here is your mother." From that time on, this disciple took her into his home.' (Jn 19:25-27)

Despite the physical pain of crucifixion, despite the spiritual pain of desertion from his Heavenly Father, despite the emotional pain from his scattered disciples - the Son of God thought of others, especially the future provision of his mother.

What a Son! What a Saviour! She cared for Him, He cared for her. Don't let your own personal battles stop you from being a public blessing.

APRIL

1st April

'For the wisdom of this world is foolishness to God.' (1 Cor. 3:19)

Being a 'fool for Christ' involves listening to the Spirit and not society, obeying the Word and not the world, trusting your faith in God and not your feelings, following Christ and not the latest craze.

2nd April

'When they came to the border of Mysia, their plan was to enter Bithynia, but the Spirit of Jesus blocked them...then they went to Troas and onto Macedonia...' (Acts 16:7-9)

Any missional endeavour needs both a **strategy** of man and the **Spirit** of God's direction - a human **plan** and divine **providence**. Like two blades on a pair of scissors, they somehow work together to bring us to our 'Macedonia' - the centre of God's will and the safest and most satisfying place on Earth.

3rd April

LESSONS FROM A SHEPHERD TO A PASTOR (Part 1)

'He calls his sheep by name.' (Jn 10:3)

I am told the Eastern shepherd delights to give names to certain sheep in his flock and if there are not too many, to all. He knows and names them according to certain characteristics or personalities they possess. They are known by **name** and not by **number.**

Pastor, how well do we know the sheep entrusted to us?

4th April

LESSONS FROM A SHEPHERD TO A PASTOR (Part 2)

'And when he puts forth his own sheep, he goes before them.' (Job 10:4)

The Eastern shepherd never drives his sheep as does the Western shepherd. He always leads them. Sometimes he leads from the front, sometimes from the side and sometimes from behind where he can gather the stragglers and protect from a sly attack from a wild animal. Butchers **drive**, leaders **lead.**

Pastor, do our people trust us enough to follow or do we drive them into their destiny?

5th April

LESSONS FROM A SHEPHERD TO A PASTOR (Part 3)

'He leads me in the right paths...' (Ps. 23:3)

The capability of the Eastern shepherd is clearly seen when they guide the entire flock through very narrow paths. Often these narrow ways are between crops that are growing and therefore forbidden. Should a sheep stray and eat from such a field, the shepherd would need to pay damages to the owner. True shepherds are **skilled**.

Pastor, how equipped are we to guide our people into fertile fields and away from forbidden fields?

6th April

LESSONS FROM A SHEPHERD TO A PASTOR (Part 4)

'I have gone astray like a lost sheep, seek your servant.' (Ps. 119:176)

It is vital that straying sheep are restored as soon as possible and not allowed to be separated from the rest of the flock. On their

own sheep are utterly helpless and bewildered as they have no sense of locality and are prone to attack.
True shepherds care just as much about the stray **one** as they do about the safe **ninety-nine.**

Pastor, be concerned about the **restoration** of current sheep as well as the **recruitment** of new ones.

7th April
LESSONS FROM A SHEPHERD TO A PASTOR (Part 5)

'They will come in and go out and find pasture.' (Jn 10:9)

The role of the shepherd is to not only feed the sheep when they are young, sick or unable to feed themselves but, ideally, to lead them to places and pastures where they can feed themselves on a regular basis. The shepherd will **lead** to the place where they can **feed.**

Pastor, do we just 'spoon-feed' the flock entrusted to us each Sunday or equip them to nourish themselves on a daily basis?

8th April
LESSONS FROM A SHEPHERD TO A PASTOR (Part 6)

'You anoint my head with oil...' (Ps. 23:5)

I am told that an enemy of the sheep is not only the obvious - the wolf, lion or bear - but especially the small and unseen insects and flies that seek to bring discomfort and disease. In order to both heal and repel against such bugs, the shepherd will place oil on certain parts of the sheep to provide much needed relief and protection.

Pastor, the members of our flock are under attack, often by the small and unseen rather than the large and obvious. Spend time with each - anointing and praying against all that 'bugs' - the flesh, the world and 'Beelzebub' himself - the Lord of the Flies!

9th April

LESSONS FROM A SHEPHERD TO A PASTOR (Part 7)

'...to put with my sheepdogs...' (Job 30:1)

At times, when a flock was particularly large, the Eastern shepherd would employ help from sheepdogs who would come behind and before the sheep leading them into their destination - the sheep pen. In the Christian life there are two sheepdogs employed to serve us named 'Goodness' and 'Mercy' who actively pursue us all the days of our life, or even 'hunt us down' - eventually leading us to our destination - 'dwelling in the house of the Lord forever.' (Ps. 23:6)

Pastor, though sheep are stubborn, they stray and often get stranded - always employ the two timeless virtues of Goodness and Mercy in your ministry. May they forever go behind and before.

10th April

'Who are you Lord?' (Acts 22:8)

'What would you have me do?" (Acts 22:10)

Notice the order of Saul's questions. We will only truly **do** when we truly **know**. Achievements for Him will follow acknowledgement of Him. '...the people that know their God shall be strong and do exploits.' (Dan. 11:32)

11th April

As New Testament believers there's two sacrifices we are to offer to God:

- Our praise, or the fruit of our **lips** (Heb. 13:15) and
- Ourselves, or the fruit of our **lives** (Rom. 12:1).

God doesn't want you on the throne of self but on the altar of sacrifice! The problem with being 'living sacrifices' is that we tend to crawl from where we should be to where we want to be.

12th April

'Do you have a right to be angry about the vine?......Should I not be concerned about that great city?' (Jon. 4:9, 11)

The man of God was concerned about a plant, whereas God, Himself, is always concerned about lost people.

Life is too short to major on the minors! His agenda needs our sole attention.

13th April

LOVE IS ALL YOU NEED!

"Yes, Lord,' he said, 'you know that I love you.' Jesus said, 'Feed my lambs." (Jn 21:15)

Everything we do for Christ has to come from our love for Christ. A striving for platforms, prestige and power will leave us perturbed. Love is not only a feeling, it's foundational. Love may not be our primary message but it is our greatest motivation. In order to be effective for Christ, Simon Peter needed to learn that duty follows devotion and never the other way around. Responsibility follows relationship! The challenge of commitment to Christ was repeated three times around a charcoal fire, not only to cancel out Peter's thrice failure around a charcoal fire (Jn 18:18), but to hammer home a vital point. How could Peter soon preach with power at Pentecost? How could Peter take the gospel to the undeserving gentiles? How could he endure prison and persecution? How could Peter eventually be crucified on a cross as predicted by Christ? By love - love for Jesus, love of himself and love for God's world.

As another great apostle was soon to discover, 'Christ's love compels us' (2 Cor. 5:14) and that, 'Without love, we gain nothing' (1 Cor.13:3).

Know the foundation of love, then you can function in love!

14th April

Never underestimate the ministry of a child. In Scripture, we see kids:

- Showing Samson's hands to the pillars (Jud. 16:26) - LEADERSHIP
- Suggesting to Naaman where to find healing (2 Kings 5:2ff) - WISDOM
- Sharing their food (Jn 6:9) - GENEROSITY
- Sensitivity to God's voice (1 Sam. 3:4) – DISCERNMENT

Children are not only a vital part of the Church's future, they're very much part of the Church's present.

15th April

Often when we read the Book of Acts we can think that there were several miracles a day and every day. Such a viewpoint of the 1st century can make us feel a failure in the 21st century if extraordinary events seem a rare occurrence. Although, when it comes to present-day miracles, I am a continuationist and not a cessationist, we need to bear in mind that Dr Luke's account covers a 30-35 year period and contains the highlights. What were God's people doing in between the signs and wonders? Sacrificially serving despite horrendous hardship.

In the midst of the **miracles** there is always the **mundane**. Faithfulness in the latter may see the fruit of the former.

16th April

'From Issachar, men who understood the times and knew what Israel should do' (1 Chron. 12:32)

Church leader, have one eye on the **world** and one eye in the **Word**. Knowing how the latter affects the former will bring **wisdom.**

17th April

'Tell me, what do you have in your house?' (2 Kings 4:2)

'...stand firm and see the deliverance the Lord will give you.' (2 Chron. 20:17)

God is a miracle-working God, that is beyond dispute. However, there are some miracles that He wants you to be a part of and some where He wants you to do nothing, but wait. Wisdom helps us to know the difference. We are often more content with the former and mistakenly believe that in some strange way our important involvement will speed up God's hand. We have more problems with the latter - waiting or standing firm is such hard work! We need to remember that much is achieved in the interim period between promise and fulfilment - that is where faith germinates and grows and without true faith it will always be impossible to please God. However, in our 'instant generation' and with our 'last minute dot com' lifestyles, waiting is unnecessary and a waste of time. Such an attitude causes us to step into miracles that God never wanted us to be a part of and like Abraham, 'Ishmaels' are born before 'Isaacs' and the former have a habit of staying around to haunt us, even after lessons are eventually learnt.

For you today, it's in the waiting. We grow in the gap!

18th April

According to Dr Luke, praises to God can be:

Spoken (Lk. 2:13)
Shouted (Lk. 19:37)
Sung (Lk. 1:46-47)

By:
Humans (Lk. 2:28)
Heavenly hosts (Lk. 2:13)

In:
Public (Lk. 1:64-65)
Private (Lk. 10:21)

Where?:
Indoors (Lk. 24:53)
Outdoors (Lk. 19:37)

When?
Circumstantial (Lk. 19:37)
Continually (Lk. 24:53)

Today, what's our excuse not to praise? If we are silent, 'the very stones will cry out!' (Lk. 19:40)

19th April

Although it has been over 500 years since 'The Protestant Reformation' broke out, could it be that some of God's people are still trying to justify themselves instead of resting in the fact that they are justified by faith alone? There is the 'power to perform,' the need to 'make our mark' and the 'striving for success' that not only grips the world but has also gained momentum in Christ's Church. Although there has always been a place for working hard and having a measure of ambition in the 'rat race' that we find ourselves, as God's people we should always remember that justification and favour before our Master is never a matter of **trying** but always one of **trusting**. The former is religion, the latter is relationship. Achievements come from our acceptance by Him. Our behaviour comes from belonging to and belief in Him. Long-lasting fruit will come from our faith in Him. We weren't saved by works, we aren't being saved by works and we won't finally be saved by works. It's grace from first to last!

Perhaps, some of us need a personal revelation of a personal 'Reformation'.

20th April

'REGRETS? I'VE HAD A FEW!'

'....he will cast our sins into the depths of the sea.' (Mic. 7:19)

I read recently of yet another celebrity who said and did something 'unwise' in their youth in the 1970s and now that some comments made over 40 years ago, arguably out of context, have resurfaced there are calls for 'cancellation' and 'ostracism'. A community so eager to embrace you can be quick to exclude you!

Although there are consequences in the natural, when there is genuine remorse and restitution, can people never be granted the grace to learn from past attitudes and actions and move on? Is anyone without regret? Those who live in glass houses should not throw stones.

I am so glad that as a Christ-follower my past mistakes, made either intentionally or in ignorance, have not be forgotten by the Lord but chosen not to be remembered by Him. They are removed by His blood and buried in the deepest sea where he has displayed a 'No Fishing!' sign for others to ignore at their peril.

Where there is true recognition and repentance, let the community show horizontal grace. Why? Because we have all been shown vertical grace.

21st April

'Do nothing out of selfish ambition or vain conceit. Rather, in humility value others above yourselves.' (Phil. 2:3)

It's not necessarily wrong to be ambitious - but strive for **servant** ambition not **selfish** ambition. When we strive for what's on God's heart, our own hearts will be satisfied in the process.

22nd April

'....not laying again the foundation of repentance from acts that lead to death, and of faith in God, instruction about cleansing rites, the laying on of hands...' (Heb. 6:1-2)

Pentecostals are not only known for the raising of their hands, but also for the laying on of their hands. However, such a truth should not be familiar to a certain denomination only but it should be foundational to the Church as a whole. According to the New Testament, we are to lay our hands on:

- The **sick** - for divine healing (Mk. 16:18)
- The **believer** - for Spirit filling (Acts 8:17)
- The **called** - for mission sending (Acts 13:3)

- The **Church** - for gift impartation (2 Tim. 1:6)

Don't just lift your hands, lay on your hands!

23rd April

'But Shammah took his stand in the middle of the field. He defended it and struck the Philistines down, and the Lord brought about a great victory.' (2 Sam. 23:12)

Scripture doesn't give us much information about this lentil field - its size, shape and significance - but I'm sure it wasn't perfect and contained the odd weed and stone. Why did this man of valour risk his life against all the odds to protect it? Not only was it a source of food for God's people, but more importantly, he protected it, because it belonged to his people - it was theirs.

Even though there is wisdom in choosing our battles, there are some wars that can never be delegated to another warrior. There are priceless 'fields' worth defending - a friendship, a marriage, your kids, your thought life, your ministry, your church. The enemy of your soul has no good plans for such things. Don't expect someone else to come riding over the hill to defend them - if not you, then who? If not now, then when?

Don't let the enemy steal your harvest. Stand at your post and declare, 'Not on my watch!'

24th April

'Ask and it shall be given to you, seek and you shall find, knock and the door will be opened to you.' (Matt. 7:7)

Jesus' commands of 'ask, seek, knock' are given in the present continuous tense and not as one-off past actions. The commands to the disciples then and now is to pray and keep on praying, seek and keep on seeking, knock and keep on knocking... until the breakthrough comes or the Lord says otherwise.

PUSH through today! Pray Until Something Happens!

25th April

'But Eleazar stood his ground and struck down the Philistines till his hand grew tired and froze to the sword.' (2 Sam. 23:10)

In the battles of life may our hands be firmly gripped to the 'sword of the Spirit, which is the word of God' (Eph. 6:17). God says it, I believe it, that settles it!

26th April

'And Benaiah was a valiant man, a doer of great deeds; he went down and slew a lion in a pit on a snowy day.' (1 Chron. 11:22)

Benaiah faced the worst possible foe (a powerful lion) in the worst possible place (a restricted pit) under the worst possible conditions (a snowy day)...yet he won!
Today, your foe may be debt, disease or disillusionment, your place may be dark and damp, your conditions and circumstances may be dire...but through Christ they can certainly be defeated!

Paul faced a powerful enemy called persecution in a restricted place called prison...yet such things could not stop him from fulfilling God's plan and purpose for his life. He could do all the things that God wanted him to do 'through Christ who gives me strength' (Phil. 4:13).

Lion? Pit? Snowy day? No problem!

27th April

'Now, Lord, consider their threats and enable your servants to speak your word with great boldness.' (Acts 4:29)

When threatened, the early Church did not pray for release **from** persecution but the courage to preach more enthusiastically **in** persecution. Sometimes we pray to escape that which God wants us to endure. We are never promised peace without problems but peace despite problems. We are not immune from pressures, we are involved in pressure!

28th April

'But God showed his great love for us by sending Christ to die for us while we were still sinners.' (Rom. 5:8)

True love is not only spoken, it has to be shown. Love is not so much a passive noun but an active verb - not merely a belief but a behaviour. It starts in the heart and has to work its way out through our hands. An attitude that soon leads to action.

Realise today, God's love for you is present continuous. He not only demonstrated it through His death at Calvary, He continues to parade it in the present - through the everyday circumstances of life.

His love for you is not rationed - it's relentless!

29th April

'But when he saw the wind, he was afraid and, beginning to sink, cried out, 'Lord, save me!" (Matt. 14:30)

When Jesus calls you out, keep looking at the Saviour, never the storm! When you step out for Him, He steps in for you! He always keeps those He calls.

30th April

'Jesus, full of the Holy Spirit, left the Jordan and was led by the Spirit into the wilderness to be tested...' (Lk. 4:1)

Often we end up in the wilderness because of wrong-doing. Incorrect choices usually carry consequences despite Heaven's forgiveness. Sometimes, however, we are led by the Spirit into the same wilderness because it's God's will. We haven't particularly done anything sinful, God just wants to sift us before he can shift us. Wisdom helps us to both know the difference and also to ask that difficult question - 'Lord, what lessons can I learn?'

Be rest assured, testing is temporary. At the end, like Jesus himself, may we know God's strengthening and return full of the Spirit.

MAY

1st May

'So he ran ahead and climbed a sycamore-fig tree to see him.' (Lk. 19:4)

To see Jesus, Zacchaeus had to change his seat. A change in position will often bring a change in perception.

In what ways do you need to adjust today in order to see Christ more clearly?

2nd May

'The Lord our God said to us at Horeb, 'You have stayed long enough at this mountain. Break camp and advance...'' (Deut. 1:6-7)

For God's people, leaving the slavery of Egypt seemed to be enough. They were given God's precepts at Sinai, provision in the wilderness and the Lord's guiding presence in the day and at night - what more could they need? They began to pitch their tents, got some roots down and believed they had arrived into God's plan and purpose - but the message was clear...Horeb was not the final destination but merely a place to 'refuel.'

Contentment is a wonderful thing but it can often produce comfort which in turn breeds contempt. Don't settle for what is just enough - a land flowing with 'milk and honey' awaits a few days hence.

3rd May

'Now an angel of the Lord said to Philip, "Go south to the road—the desert road—that goes down from Jerusalem to Gaza." So he started out, and on his way he met an Ethiopian...' (Acts 8:26-27)

Although the instructions of God may not always make sense, we need to obey His voice before the opportunity presents itself visually. Position yourself and wait for the promise to be fulfilled!

4th May

'It takes eleven days to go from Horeb to Kadesh Barnea...' (Deut. 1:2)

Sadly, a journey to the Promised Land that should have taken God's people a matter of days ended up taking a number of years. Learning the lessons of **faith** over the giants will enable us to possess our 'Promised Land' quicker. Living in f**ear** of the giants will always slow us down!

5th May
OPPORTUNITY KNOCKS!

'The wind blows wherever it pleases.' (Jn 3:8)

The word 'opportunity' comes from the Latin phrase, *ob portum veniens* - "coming toward a port" which refers to a favourable wind blowing ships into the harbour.

May the wind of God's Spirit blow you into His plan and purpose today!

6th May

'Open my eyes that I may see wonderful things in your word.' (Ps. 119:18)

Naturally speaking, digging to find treasure takes time. However, the enthusiasm for the end result more than compensates for the effort. As with the natural, so with the spiritual. To find both treasure and truth in God's word takes time. The Apostle Paul uses such words as 'do your best' and 'worker' in the same sentence as 'word of truth' (2 Tim. 2:15). There is often perspiration before revelation!

Make it a habit to dig deep into Scripture and you will find it digs deep into you...by the Spirit. Read it slowly, read it curiously, read it often.

7th May
BROKEN BEFORE BEAUTY!

'The woman broke the jar of perfume and poured it over Jesus...this

is a beautiful thing' (Mk 14:3,6)

Before the Lord could receive the costly act of devotion, a breaking had to take place.

True worth-ship will cost more to the giver than the receiver! Once the jar was broken it became total - there was no saving some for another time or another place.

Before we worship today, before we pour out all to Him, may we be truly broken before the Master. Pour out all today to the One who poured out all for us.

This, to Him, is a beautiful thing!

8th May

'And having disarmed the powers and authorities, he made a public spectacle of them, triumphing over them by the cross.' (Col. 2:15)

When the powerful Roman Empire conquered a nation, it would parade a number of its prisoners through the streets where they experienced public shame and defeat. For the conqueror - honour! For the conquered - humiliation!

The Church's 'VE Day' was 2000 years ago. The enemy was utterly defeated and his most powerful weapons - sin and death - rendered powerless. However, many in God's army haven't heard the good news of total victory over the enemy of our souls and act as though the war still needs winning.

Live as a victor not a victim! You are on the side that is not merely winning - but has already won. We are not only conquerors but more than conquerors!

9th May

Every time Mary of Bethany is mentioned in Scripture she is found at Jesus' feet:

Listening - Diligence (Lk. 10:39)
Questioning - Doubt (Jn 11:32)
Worshipping - Devotion (Jn 12:3)

Wherever we are in our walk with Him, spend time at His feet!

10th May

MIRACLE AT THE POOL (Part 1)

"Do you want to be made well?" asked Jesus. "Sir," the invalid replied, "I have no one to help me into the pool when the water is stirred. While I am trying to get in, someone else goes down ahead of me." (Jn 5:7)

Notice, when asked if he wanted a miracle, the disabled man blames someone else.

Often our breakthrough begins when our excuses end!

11th May

MIRACLE AT THE POOL (Part 2)

"Sir," the invalid replied, "I have no one to help me into the pool when the water is stirred." (Jn 5:7)

Many around the pool tried to get to the water. For one needy soul, the Living Water (Jer. 2:13) went to him!

Religion is when we try to race to the pool. Grace is when God comes to us!

12th May

MIRACLE AT THE POOL (Part 3)

'Jesus said to him, 'Do you want to be healed?'' (Jn 5:6)

Notice, Jesus did not say to the disabled man, 'Do you want to feel better?'

The Lord doesn't want us to be comfortable for now, He wants us to be changed forever!

13th May

'In the presence of God...I give you this charge...' (2 Tim. 4:1)

The presence of the Lord is not only to be found in a place of worship but in a prison of woe. It is there, not only in a sanctuary of many but in the solitude of one.

For the countless number imprisoned for their faith today - may you know His presence.

14th May

"If I have cheated anybody out of anything, I will pay back four times the amount." (Lk. 19:8)

After receiving forgiveness from God, true repentance should include restitution with others. We not only turn our back on sin, we also turn towards those we have wronged. Repentance means taking responsibility!

15th May

'He appointed twelve that they might be with him and that he might send them out to preach.' (Mk 3:14)

According to this verse, there were two reasons Jesus chose His first disciples. The second reason was for them to **do for Him**, the first reason was for them to **be with Him**.

Duty for God will come from our devotion to God. From relationship comes responsibility!

16th May

'And who knows but that you have come to your royal position for such a time as this.' (Est. 4:14)

To reach the precise position of your divine destiny, don't rely on horizontal human networking but rather on vertical heavenly navigation. Like God's people in the time of Esther, not only will you benefit, others will be blessed as well.

17th May

'Nathan replied to the king, "Whatever you have in mind, go ahead and do it, for the Lord is with you." But that night the word of the Lord came to Nathan, saying:
"Go and tell my servant David, 'This is what the Lord says: Are you the one to build me a house to dwell in?" (2 Sam. 7:3-5)

Within a short space of time, the prophet Nathan went from speaking his own mind, 'Go and build it' - to speaking God's mind, 'Are you the one to build?' It's so easy, even in our zeal and wanting to help, to confuse the two - what God has said and what we think.

Let's be careful when we add 'thus sayeth the Lord' to our declarations. Bringing the Lord's name into it doesn't let us off the hook, it brings both our and God's integrity into question.

18th May

'How God anointed Jesus with the Holy Ghost and with power and he went about doing good...' (Acts 10:38)

Are we going about doing good or are we just going about?

19th May

'With his wife's full knowledge he kept back part of the money for himself, but brought the rest and put it at the apostles' feet.' (Acts 5:2)

The story of Ananias and Sapphira is one that is sobering, yet misunderstood. What was their crime warranting a dramatic death? Did they not give enough to God? Did they short-change the early Church community? The issue was not about how much they gave or held back, it was not about the actions of their hands but the attitude of their hearts. They gave a proportion of the proceeds of selling their property - this is not the problem, this is wise and responsible. Scripture expects us to give a proportion of our income (1 Cor. 16:2) and even the saintly Levite Barnabas, though he sold land and gave all, had another piece of land that he kept to pass on as an inheritance (Lev. 25:34). There is a place for being generous yet responsible in our giving. The underlying problem with Ananias and Sapphira is that they gave a proportion but acted as though they'd given all. There were lies and dishonesty in abundance.

God is not an accountant in the sky. He's not concerned about the exact amount we give but the attitude with which we give. Are we generous or greedy? Do we give bountifully or begrudgingly? Do we wish to be approved by God or applauded by man?

What's in our hearts is more important than what's in our hands.

20th May

'After that, he poured water into a basin and began to wash his disciples' feet...' (Jn 13:5)

'Instead, one of the soldiers pierced Jesus' side with a spear, bringing a sudden flow of blood and water'. (Jn 19:34)

Before Gethsemane, Jesus washed His disciples' feet - Servant!

On Golgotha His blood washed away our sin - Saviour!

21st May

'The Lord said to Gideon, 'You have too many men. I cannot deliver Midian into their hands, or Israel would boast against me saying, 'My own strength has saved me.''' (Jud. 7:2)

The battle against the Midianites was always to be one of **faith** more than **fortitude**. For God's people, it was never to be about matching the size and strength of the enemy so that man would get promoted but purposely cutting it back so that the heavenly Miracle-worker would be praised.

If the Lord is bringing a cutting back and a stripping away in our lives it is so that a watching world will eventually marvel - not at your achievements but at God's abilities through you!

Like Gideon, He often places us in impossible situations so that the God of the possible can be made known.

22nd May

'Religion that God our Father accepts as pure and faultless is this: to look after orphans and widows in their distress...' (Jam. 1:27)

Being truly spiritual involves being truly practical. It may start in the head and heart but has to work its way out through our hands.

23rd May

'Then Peter got down out of the boat, walked on the water and came toward Jesus.' (Matt. 14:29)

True faith can never be fully exercised at the back of the boat, only on the surface of the sea.

24th May

'Therefore go and make disciples of all nations…' (Matt. 28:19)

The 'Great Commission' is simple: To see the whole gospel, proclaimed to the whole world by the whole Church. May it never become the 'Great Omission!'

25th May

'Jesus called to him those he wanted…' (Mk 3:13)

Be careful who you let into your life and how far you let them in. Build your relationships like the tabernacle. Have an:

-Outer court
-Inner Court
-Sanctuary

Remember, though Jesus loved and used them all, He still had the 'Seventy-two' (Lk. 10:1), the 'Twelve' (Mk 3:14) and the 'Three' (Matt. 17:1). There are simply levels and layers of relationship you can have with one group, that you can't have with the others.

Be at peace with that!

26th May

'Your word is a lamp for my feet, a light on my path.' (Ps. 119:105)

Scripture is a lamp not a floodlight. Often the Lord gives enough light for the next step on life's journey, not for the whole of the path.

27th May

'The waters were divided and the Israelites went through on dry ground...' (Ex. 14:21-22)

'As soon as they set foot in the Jordan its waters will be divided...' (Jos. 3:13)

Notice, in both situations the 'waters were divided'. However, sometimes the Lord makes a clear way before we step out, sometimes we step out before there's a clear way. Faith and obedience are needed for both!

28th May

NEIGHBOUR OR NEMESIS?

'They forsook the Lord, who had brought them out of Egypt. They followed and worshiped various gods of the peoples around them. They aroused the Lord's anger.' (Jud. 2:12)

Once in Canaan, the Israelites failed to expel their foes. They were out of Egypt, but Egypt was not yet out of them. The former was a procedure, the latter a process. Our immediate salvation should always be followed by a longer period of sanctification and a large part of this is driving out from our hearts and minds those things which are displeasing to the Lord and damaging to us. Unfortunately, all too often, we allow such 'enemies' to continue dwelling in our midst - they become welcome neighbours instead of an unwelcome nemesis. Their 'gods' quickly become our 'gods' and the Lord is angry.

We may be in the 'Promised Land' today but what still needs driving out? Corrupting company, unrighteous reading material, warping websites? Don't allow them to dwell any longer as their gods will soon become ours. We are in the world but never of it. Don't allow its systems and structures to squeeze you into its mould. Now that you are out of 'Egypt', through 'Red Sea baptism,' allow 'Egypt' to come out of you!

29th May

'I praise you because I am fearfully and wonderfully made...' (Ps. 139:14)

God gave you a fingerprint that no one else in this world has so that you can leave an imprint on the world that no one else can.

30th May

FAMOUS LAST WORDS!

'You shall receive power when the Holy Spirit comes upon you and you shall be my witnesses in Jerusalem, Judea and Samaria and the uttermost parts of the earth.' (Acts 1:8)

Here we see:

- The **People** given the promise - 'You...'

- The **Promise** of **Power** - 'You shall receive power when the Holy Spirit comes upon you'

- The **Purpose** of the power - 'be witnesses'

- The **Place** to witness - 'Jerusalem, Judea, Samaria and the uttermost parts of the earth'

Christ's last words should be the Church's first priority!

31st May

'I urge, then, first of all, that petitions, prayers, intercession and thanksgiving be made for all people—for kings and all those in authority, that we may live peaceful and quiet lives in all godliness and holiness. This is good, and pleases God our Saviour...' (1 Tim. 2:1-3)

Who was in power when Paul said these words to young Timothy? Either Emperors Nero or Domitian depending on when this letter is dated. Either way, both men were:

- Despots;
- Enemies of the Church;
- Unelected leaders;
- Immoral.

Paul didn't ask the Ephesian believers to pray for their removal, nor to agree with their policies and practices. There are no commands to protest...simply to pray so that 'we may live peaceful lives'. This pleases God.

JUNE

1st June

'God tested Abraham...'Take your son and sacrifice him..." (Gen. 22:1-2)

Though God does not tempt us so we may do wrong, He does test us so we may do what's right. Testing should never make us bitter but always better and it's a painful, pruning process where we determine what our priorities truly are - and what they're not.

On Mount Moriah, God never really wanted Isaac - He just wanted Abraham and the test was to see whether he would give to God that which was most precious, dear and valued. When Abraham had to choose between his earthly son and heavenly Father, who would come first?

What is our 'Isaac' - our possessions, our career, our home, car or family? These things are often God-given and not necessarily wrong, but they should never take first place. Are we willing to sacrifice them and lay all on the altar to prove our devotion to the Lord or will they remain on the throne?

Abraham showed how willing he was to go all the way and the following verses in Scripture speak of God's sure blessing and increase in his present and future, even beyond Abraham's earthly days!

Obedience and faith, though costly at times, leads to overwhelming favour!

2nd June

'David replied, 'I have sinned against the Lord!" (2 Sam. 12:13)

Integrity may be lost when we sin against the Lord, but we can start to get it back when we are quick to acknowledge our wrong before others. Integrity is never irretrievable!

3rd June

BAD DECISIONS

'If any of you lacks wisdom, you should ask God...' (Jam. 1:5)

When I think about my life I find that I have made the worst decisions when one of these dynamics is at work in my heart:

-When I get impatient and I have to have it now;

-When I am afraid and react to my circumstances instead of responding courageously;

-When I am angry and I let my feelings dictate my decisions instead of waiting to calm down;

-When I am jealous of someone and compete, instead of completing the person;

- When I am not feeling good about myself and I **do** things to feel better about me instead of
  listening to who God says I am;

-When I feel pressured to make a decision before I am ready;

-When I feel rejected by someone and I work to build a case against them instead of loving them
  anyway;

-Most importantly, when I don't take time to listen to God's perspective on my situations.

Hate the eight!

4th June

'Jabez cried out to the God of Israel, "Oh, that you would bless me and enlarge my territory! Let your hand be with me, and keep me

from harm so that I will be free from pain." And God granted his request.' (1 Chron. 4:10)

Jabez did not allow the pain from his past to deter him from taking hold of God's blessings in the present. He audaciously asked for and received:

- **Promotion** of blessing – 'Oh, that you would bless me'
- **Propagation** of influence – 'enlarge my territory'
- **Presence** and **power** of God – 'Let your hand be with me'
- **Protection** from danger – 'keep me from harm'

Don't let your history determine your destiny! The blessings of God belong to you as much as the next person. Make Jabez's prayer your own.

5th June

'But the father said to his servants, 'Quick! Bring the best robe and put it on him. Put a ring on his finger and sandals on his feet.'' (Lk. 15:22)

After the American Civil War, President Lincoln was asked how he would now treat the 'rebellious southern states'. His reply was profound, 'I'll treat them just as if they'd never rebelled in the first place'.

When we make a decision to repent and return to the Father, we are justified. He sees me just-as-if-I'd never rebelled in the first place. Waiting for us is the best robe of righteousness, a ring of authority and sandals of sonship!

6th June

'This was not revealed to you by man but by my Father in heaven.....on this rock I will build my church..' (Matt. 16:17-18)

Church is established, enlarged and enhanced after personal, heavenly **revelation** and not public, earthly **information!**

Jesus said, 'I will send my Spirit' and He has. He said, 'I will come again' and He will. He said, 'I will build my Church' and He is.

7th June

THINGS JESUS NEVER SAID (Part 1)

'Do what makes you happy!'

Contrary to the 'American Dream' the disciple of Christ's ultimate pursuit is not 'happiness' but 'holiness' (1 Pet. 1:16). However, when we are holy we are then happy. True contentment is not found in what self wants, but what the Saviour wants.

8th June

THINGS JESUS NEVER SAID (Part 2)

'Feeding these people will cause a dependency culture!'

When Jesus fed the hungry it was to meet an immediate need (Lk 9:13) not anticipate where it could possibly lead.

Help someone today because it's the right thing to do!

9th June

THINGS JESUS NEVER SAID (Part 3)

'I will only heal you if you follow me!'

When the Lord performs a miracle in us and for us, there are no strings attached. No spiritual 'blackmail'. We follow Christ because we want to, not because we have to. Relationship not religion!

10th June

'Build houses, settle down, plant gardens and eat what they produce...marry and have sons, increase in number and seek the peace and prosperity of the city to which I have carried you into exile...' (Jer. 29:5-7)

Like the exiled people of God, often the most difficult task we face in our Christian lives is truly accepting the place where He has led us, to be grateful for our 'lot' in life. We are all guilty of 'looking over the wall' - 'Why am I not further ahead in my career at this stage of my life? Why is my car older than my neighbour's car? Why am I plagued with health problems when others seem fighting fit? After all, isn't the grass greener on the other side of the fence?' It may appear greener, but that's because it's often artificial.

Whatever place you find yourself in today, if God has led you, accept it and settle down. Seek to be productive in your corner of the 'vineyard' and plant. Share your faith and reproduce spiritual children. Pray for and be a blessing to your community, that it may truly prosper.

Faithfulness will lead to fruitfulness in any setting. Acceptance of His will always results in abundance!

Be constructive in the place God has led you don't be critical of where He has led you.

11th June

'Esau gave up his birthright for a pot of stew' (Gen. 25:34)

In moments of temporary physical hunger don't lose that which satisfies the spirit permanently.

Succumbing to a short temptation of the carnal in the present, can cause us to live in the long term consequences in the future.

12th June

'Let us throw off everything that hinders...' (Heb. 12:1)

Notice, who does the throwing off? Not God but us. We can often put the responsibility for casting off habits and hindrances on the **Spirit** when the onus is on **self.**

If you want to soar you have to get rid of what weighs you down!

13th June

'I have come to do your will O God.' (Heb. 10:7)

Be careful how you measure success in God's Kingdom. If it's measured by how far we travel, how many followers we have, how much money is in the bank, how many qualifications we earn or books we write then Jesus, Himself, was unsuccessful during His earthly ministry.

I remember hearing an elderly man tell me how he had spent his life climbing the 'ladder of success' only to realise at the end it was leaning against the wrong wall.

True spiritual success for the spiritual man and woman is finding the plan of God for our individual lives and serving faithfully to the finish.

Are we pursuing God's full will or pandering to the world's empty expectations?

14th June

'Those who belong to Jesus have crucified the flesh...' (Gal. 5:24)

Don't seek to cast out what should be regularly crucified!

Often the problem in our lives is not Satan but self.

15th June

'Be transformed by the renewing of your mind, then you will be able to test and approve what God's will is...' (Rom. 12:2)

The Lord has provided everything we need in order to know His will - advice from other **saints**, the **Scriptures**, **situations**, the **Spirit** and especially our common **sense**. They all work together in cooperation, not competition!

16th June

'They devoted themselves to fellowship...' (Acts 2:42)

True biblical fellowship, or *koinonia,* is community and communion, participation and partnership. It's about sharing our treasure, time and talents with others. *Koinonia* is generosity and goodness, being practical not theoretical. It has more to do with the outworking through our hands than what we think in our heads. It has little to do with belief and everything to do with behaviour. There is a time to clasp our hands together and pray for others but there are also too many missed opportunities when those same hands needed to get dirty in our service to others. We should pray and be practical! Christ was a man of prayer and still is - but he was also practical by feeding the hungry, healing the sick and touching the leper. He was helpful in times of hurt.

Fellowship is so much more than superficial socialising or even attendance at Sunday services. We are 'fellows in the same ship!' Your storm is my storm! Your journey is my journey!

17th June

'I have seen the oppression of my people...I have heard their groaning and have come down to set them free.' (Acts 7:34)

Not only is God aware of our plight, He acts in response to our plight. He recognises and reacts!

18th June

'Then the sailors said, 'Come, let us cast lots to find out who is responsible for this calamity we are in..." (Jon. 1:7)

Other people can suffer when we make incorrect decisions. A lack of obedience will not only affect ourselves but those around us and those who come after us.

19th June

'But David encouraged himself in the Lord his God.' (1 Sam. 30:6)

I am a strong proponent of encouraging one another as much as possible. There is certainly a place for meaningful fellowship in its various forms. But what happens when you have no one to turn to on a horizontal level - when, perhaps, like David even your closest allies have turned against you and are reaching for the stones? What do you do when you quickly move from doing nothing wrong to doing nothing right, from hero to zero? This is the exact time to reach out to One on a vertical level. We find our ultimate strength in the Lord through:

- The **Word** - remembering His promises over our lives;

- **Worship** - reminding ourselves of who He is;

- **Work** - resuming the task He has already given us to do.

In the valley and on the mountaintop, turn to the One who never turns against you!

20th June

'Jesus was asleep in the stern of the boat' (Mk 4:38)

'Jonah went below deck and fell asleep' (Jon. 1: 5)

Better to find true rest in the centre of God's will than to try to sleep in a storm of disobedience.

21st June

'Love one another' (Jn 13:34)

'Love one another' (Jn 13:35)

'Love one another' (Jn 15:12)

'Love one another' (Jn 15:17)

'Love one another' (Rom. 12:10)

'Love one another' (1 Thess. 3:12)

'Love one another' (1 Pet. 1:22)

Got the message?

22nd June

'Until the time came to fulfill his dreams, the LORD tested Joseph's character.' (Ps. 105:19)

Being tested? You're in company with the best.

Before God does a work through you he has to do a work in you.

Before promotion there has to be purification.

Before breakthrough there are some battles.

Before a shifting in your circumstances there has to be a sifting in your character.

Before we are trusted by God we have to be tested by God.

23rd June

'Without faith it is impossible to please God...' (Heb. 11:6)

God never gives you a dream that matches your budget. He's not checking your bank account, He's checking your faith!

24th June

'In the year that King Uzziah died, I saw the Lord, high and exalted, seated on a throne....then I heard the voice of the Lord saying, 'Whom shall I send?'' (Is. 6:1, 8)

King Uzziah reigned over Judah for some 52 years and brought relative stability to the nation at that time. His death, therefore, caused great unease to the people with fear of the future and uncertainty in the present. However, at this time of instability two things happened - something was **seen** and something was **heard**. Whatever the circumstances on Earth, the Lord, the one true King, was still on the throne in Heaven and a clear commission was given to the prophet - a call to **respond.**

As our world continues to be in crisis, may God's people in every nation make a covenant to **see**, **hear** and then **respond** to what they see and hear. May we see His true position as Ruler of all and may this quickly be followed by hearing our purpose in this nation - to bring God's word of eternal hope.

Recognising, receiving and reacting should always come together.

25th June

'Give me this mountain that the Lord has promised...' (Josh. 14:12)

Though some mountains in our lives are problems which need to be conquered, some are promises which need to be claimed. Such promises need to be:

- **Personal** - 'Give me'
- **Specific** - 'this'
- **Sizeable** – 'mountain'
- **God-given** - 'the Lord has promised'

What has God promised you in days gone by? May the promise soon become your possession.

26th June

'We do not know what to do but our eyes are on you.' (2 Chron. 20:12)

'He does not take his eyes off the righteous....' (Job 36:7)

Though our eyes are to be fixed on the Lord, His eyes are fixed on us!

27th June

CONTEXT IS KEY! (Part 1)

'I can do all this through Christ who gives me strength.' (Phil. 4:13)

There are many popular Bible verses that we like to 'name, claim and frame'...quite literally! Such verses as Philippians 4:13 for example are found on fridge magnets, bumper stickers, body tattoos, on book marks, screen savers and 101 other places including under the eyes of a certain American football star.

This scripture, especially, is a favourite of some TV evangelists in pursuit of earthly success in every area of life and can be used as a Christian mantra or incantation when we are at the starting blocks of a race, at the bottom of a steep mountain, about to give a presentation or sit an exam. Don't get me wrong, the Lord is, indeed, our helper (Ps. 121:2) but in context this verse is talking about knowing God's strength in specific circumstances not as a blanket promise against each and every 'giant' that needs bringing down.

This verse is not really about who has the strength to play to the best of their abilities, e.g. in a sporting contest, but is rather about having strength to be content when we are facing those moments in life when physical resources are minimal.

In our interpretation of Scripture, it isn't what we intend the verse to say but what the original author intended it to say. Context is king! Context is key!

A **text** taken out of con**text** leaves you with a con!

28th June

CONTEXT IS KEY! (Part 2)

'For I know the plans I have for you...plans to prosper you and not to harm you...' (Jer. 29:11)

Here is a verse given to me in good faith by a sincere 'saint' whilst embarking on full-time ministry over 27 years ago. Again, a scripture found on graduation cards and fridges, bumper stickers and living room walls. Although, undoubtedly, such a promise has been a source of strength to the individual whilst at the crossroads of life or in the pits of despair - in context, this passage of the Bible is not really about **me**...but **we**.

The Prophet Jeremiah was writing to those about to receive a one-way ticket into exile and the generation after them. The 70+ years will be hard, away from their homeland, away from their temple, away from what was familiar. Would God forget His people? Did they feature any further in His future plans and purposes? The word of the Lord was clear. In their new and uncomfortable surroundings His people were not to mope and pine for what they no longer had. The command was to now learn to love the place they now lived, to work the land, to raise children, to be a blessing to those around. They were to be fruitful even in that which was foreign. The promise was to be fulfilled ultimately and not imminently! It was addressed to a **community** and not a specific **character** or individual! God will never forget nor forsake them and when the lessons have been learned, when His people have been purified...according to His watch and in His way He will bring them back and all will be well. In the meantime they can experience a prospering even in the midst of problems.

Although as a community of God's people on earth there is much discomfort and doom, Christ still has a plan for His Church. He will remember His Bride and ultimately all will be well. In the meantime, as His Body on earth, let's love the place we live and seek blessing to be a blessing.

29th June

CONTEXT IS KEY! (Part 3)

'And my God will supply every need of yours according to his riches in glory in Christ Jesus.' (Phil. 4:19)

To conclude the three-parter on some of the most misunderstood and misused scripture verses in the Bible.

Again, a popular verse for those of us in financial difficulty, debt and desperate need. A much-quoted promise by TV preachers to prove perfect health and wealth. A scripture found on the fridge and claimed on a daily basis.

Please, I am still a firm believer in 'standing on the promises of God' - but such promises need to be rooted in truth, the whole truth and nothing but the truth! To establish such truth, context is key.

Philippians 4:19 is not to be used as a 'proof text' snatched away and isolated from the verses preceding it. Any weird and wonderful doctrine and practice can (and unfortunately has been) 'proved' this way. Neither is it an unconditional promise, but a conditional one. God's promise to supply our needs is rooted in the context of faithful, generous and sacrificial giving by His people. God gives to those who have already given!

The Apostle Paul had thanked and commended the Philippians for their sacrificial giving to himself and his ministry on more than one occasion (v16) - especially as other assembles hadn't (v15). It was to such givers that God, Himself, will give It was to such generous people that the Lord himself will be generous.

He meets our needs to express His approval of our giving. This may sound harsh, but God does not promise to supply the needs of stingy, slothful and selfish saints!

He is and will continue to be Jehovah Jireh! However, as with most of the promises of God, we need to act first. We play our part and God plays His - not out of a sense of religion but relationship. Although our motive is to be pure and we should never 'give' to 'get' nor to treat the Lord as a heavenly ATM, although we give because we want to, we are expected to and because the Kingdom, in reality, operates through both faith and finance - when we do give to God's Kingdom in its various facets, God gives to us according to His riches! The floodgates open (Mal. 3:10), our cup overflows (Ps. 23:5 & Lk. 6:38).

30th June

'For God has not given us a spirit of fear...' (2 Tim. 1:7)

F.E.A.R. has two meanings:

Forget **E**verything **A**nd **R**un, or

Face **E**verything **A**nd **R**ise.

The choice is ours!

JULY

1st July

'And he still maintains his integrity...' (Job 2:3)

The dictionary definition of the word 'integrity' means to be 'whole' and 'undivided'. It is linked to the words 'integer' which is a whole number and 'integral' which means 'complete'. In Scripture, the word means 'to be upright in the whole of one's life' - not just publicly but personally, not only with our families but with our finances, in both our marriages and our ministries, in how we raise our children and conduct ourselves in our careers.

However, we notice from the example of Job that true integrity is not only to be gained but maintained. That's the hard bit! It can take years to get but seconds to lose. We also notice that integrity has to be tested to prove if it's genuine. It's far easier to show on the mountain top when everything falls into place, but what about in the valley when the 'chips' are down? Job showed himself to be of upright character when it mattered the most - covered in boils having lost his children and cattle.

It's a mystery of the Almighty why bad things happen to good people and why good things happen to bad people. However, we are not always called to understand God's ways but undertake God's ways. Ultimately, we may never have the answers but we do have the assurance that when 'He has tried us, we shall come forth as gold.' (Job 23:10)

2nd July

'To each is given the manifestation of the Spirit for the common good.' (1 Cor. 12:7)

Gifts given by man are meant to be kept. Gifts given by God are designed to be given away.

We are blessed to be a blessing!

3rd July

From Acts 13:1-3, we can see that the church at Antioch was:

- **Scripture** based (v1)
- **Sundry** leadership (v1)
- **Spirit** led (v2)
- **Sent** to the nations (v3)

The late, great Billy Graham was once accused of taking the contemporary Church back 50 years. 'What a shame,' he replied, 'I wanted to take it back 2000 years!'

If we don't know the Church's **history** we won't understand its **destiny!**

4th July

'Those who know your name trust in you...' (Ps. 9:10)

All around the globe this Sunday, over 1 billion believers will be coming together in a range of settings. Although each gathering will be different, with diversity in our unity, I trust that one Name will be lifted higher than all others.

The Psalmist said, 'O Lord, our Lord, how majestic is your name in all the earth!'

The angel said, 'You are to give him the name Jesus, because he will save his people from their sins.'

Jesus said, 'In my name they will drive out demons and speak in new languages...'

Peter said, 'There is no other name under heaven by which we are saved.'

Paul said, 'Therefore God exalted him to the highest place and gave him the name that is above every name...'

What a Name!

5th July

'Cast all your burdens on him because he cares for you.' (1 Pet. 5:7)

'Carry each other's burdens...' (Gal. 6:2)

In the Christian life, there are some cares we should cast and some we should carry. The Apostle Peter exhorts us to 'throw' our own burdens on the Lord - we literally get them as far from ourselves as possible, never to be retrieved. As a fisherman, Peter was used to casting his nets and throwing them as far as possible to guarantee a good catch. The Apostle Paul, on the other hand, encourages us to take on other people's burdens - when they seem unable to give them to God themselves. The picture is of a soldier wounded in battle, a colleague takes his backpack on himself and carries him to safety.

Let's not carry what we should be casting and cast what we should be carrying. Let's do both at the same time.

6th July

"He has risen! He is not here." (Mk. 16:6)

The empty tomb is more than enough to fill the empty heart.

For the disciple of Christ, it's Easter every day!

7th July

'And they took offense at him. But Jesus said to them, "A prophet is not without honour except in his own town." And he did not do many miracles there because of their lack of faith.' (Matt. 13:57-58)

Don't let familiarity with the spiritual family around you rob you of the miracles God wants to do for you through them.

Over-familiarity can kill faith! Though we get used to them, God can still use them!

8th July

'Be careful, however, that the exercise of your rights does not become a stumbling block to the weak.' (1 Cor. 8:9)

In New Testament times it was common for the meat sold in the market place to have previously been sacrificed to idols in one of the many temples in the city. Although knowing this, some believers, the Apostle Paul included, saw no problem in eating such meat. Their reasoning? Idols are not real therefore their conscience is clear. However, at the same time there were some believers who were troubled by the meat that was sacrificed before being sold. Because their conscience would not allow it, they saw consuming such meat as 'wrong' for their lives. The clear teaching of Paul is not for one side to become a stumbling block to the other. The one who views the meat as harmless should not seek to persuade the one who views the meat as harmful to partake. This would cause them to sin, not against God but against themselves.
Today, in most cultures, this particular practice of meat does not apply - however, the principle does.

With regards to such practices as a Christian consuming alcohol or shopping on a Sunday, there will be two viewpoints. There will be those who do not have a problem with a little wine or retail therapy on the Lord's Day. There will equally be those who, through their view of Scripture, tradition, upbringing etc, will have serious reservations about such practices and whose personal conscience will not allow them to partake. According to Paul, both sides should show respect to the other, even though both sides may believe they are 'right'. Although there are clear rights and wrongs according to Scripture, there are also some 'grey' areas. Let's not cause anyone to stumble in their personal journey. Remember, there is always more to unite us than divide us!

9th July

LESSONS FROM THE PIT (Part 1)

'He lifted me out of the slimy pit...' (Ps. 40:2)

When you're in a pit of despair, you can't look down, only up. The answer isn't beneath us, or around us, but above!

10th July

LESSONS FROM THE PIT (Part 2)

'He lifted me out of the slimy pit, out of the mud and mire...' (Ps. 40:2)

The trouble with a slimy pit is that the more you try to climb out in your own strength the more you slip back down. Such a person needs rescuing not religion, to keep trusting not trying, a Saviour not self-help.

11th July

LESSONS FROM THE PIT (Part 3)

'Joseph had a dream, and when he told it to his brothers, they hated him all the more.....'Throw him into this pit...'' (Gen. 37:5, 22)

In the pit, keep the dream alive! Remember what God said before you fell in. Circumstances beyond your control don't change the call.

12th July

LESSONS FROM THE PIT (Part 4)

'I sought the LORD, and he answered me; he delivered me from all my fears.' (Ps. 34:4)

Waiting in the pit can be hard as things don't move quickly. However, a waiting season doesn't have to be a wasted season. It is a time to seek the Deliverer not only our deliverance - His face and not just His hand. When we find the former, the latter often follows.

13th July

LESSONS FROM THE PIT (Part 5)

'The God of all comfort who comforts us in all our troubles, so that we can comfort those in any trouble with the comfort we ourselves re-

ceive from God.' (2 Cor. 1:3-4)

When God brings you out of the pit, don't forget those who are still there. The butler forgot Joseph when he was set free. However, true freedom should bring responsibility - to others.

14th July

PLEASED BEFORE PRODUCTION!

'The Holy Spirit descended on him in bodily form like a dove. And a voice came from heaven: 'You are my Son, whom I love; with you I am well pleased." (Lk. 3:22)

Before His ministry started in earnest, the Son of God received a reassurance from above and a resting of the Spirit upon His life. The Father confirmed how pleased He was with Jesus, but notice - it was before He performed miracles and before he preached to the masses.

Because we live in a visible results oriented world, we tend to believe that our Heavenly Father is a hard taskmaster - someone who needs to be satisfied with what we produce at the end of each day. We soon get caught on the conveyor belt of religion and works resulting in unnecessary pressure. But notice, Jesus produced from a position of already being pleasing to the Father. He didn't please God because He produced. Devotion came before duty.

Today, rest in the assurance of God's approval because of the cross of Christ. We were not saved by works and we don't continue to be saved by works - it's by grace from first to last!

15th July

'I praise you because I am fearfully and wonderfully made; your works are wonderful, I know that full well.' (Ps. 139:14)

Snowflakes are renowned for their uniqueness. No matter how many billions of them fall from the sky at any one time, there are never two the same. Every single one of the snowflakes has its own individual pattern.

If snowflakes are unique, so are you! Feel special? You should!

16th July

'Let your light shine before men; that they may see your good works, and. glorify your Father who is in heaven.' (Matt. 5:16)

There was once an argument between the wind and the sun about who was stronger than the other. They argued for a long time but neither of them emerged the winner. It wasn't too long before they spotted a man walking on the road. Looking at the man wearing a coat, an idea struck them both. They challenged each other that the one who succeeded in removing the coat from the man's back was the strongest. The wind volunteered to try first. It began to blow hard, raising gusts of air and making it harder for the man to take a step further. But, the man clutched his coat tight around him and resumed walking with great difficulty. The wind continued blowing harder and harder, but the man held on to his coat tighter and tighter. And continued his journey forward. Finally, the wind was exhausted and gave up. His efforts had been futile. It was now the turn of the sun. He looked at the man and began to gently shine upon the path the man was walking on. The man looked up at the sky – surprised at the change in weather. The sun did not spend much energy, neither did he apply any effort. He just continued shining upon the man's head gently. Soon the man was huffing and puffing, and sweating profusely. Unable to bear the rising heat, the man finally took off his coat and headed to a nearby tree to rest for a while under its shade.

We won't win the world by force, but by shining!

17th July

'As Samson approached the vineyards of Timnah, suddenly a young lion came roaring towards him. The Spirit of the Lord came upon him in power...' (Jud. 14: 5-6)

'So Samson told her everything...' (Jud. 16:17)

Like Samson, how quickly we can go from times of great faith, to moments of foolishness, from experiences in the Spirit to episodes of the flesh.

Charismatic highlights in our lives need to be matched by character consistency. Power without control means nothing. Loose cannons not only shoot themselves in the foot, but often others in the process!

18th July

'But Joseph left his garment and fled...' (Gen. 39:12)

To keep your integrity sometimes you have to leave certain things behind.

How did Joseph have the motivation to run whilst in a time of intense temptation? Why do people rise in the early hours of the morning to work out at the gym or run in the cold and rain? The answer is the same - because they have already made the decision to do so!

Let's decide in the 'light' how we will behave in the 'dark'.

19th July

'So David was brought in...then the Lord said...'He is the one..." (1 Sam. 16:12)

Although there is a very clear command in Scripture to 'walk by faith', there are times in the Christian race when we need to literally 'see' something, before we can know the mind of the Lord in a particular instance. In the above verse, Samuel had to 'see' David, before he knew he was God's chosen. It wasn't enough to know about him from a distance and from those supposedly closest to him.

At this time, you may be needing direction. My advice to you is to position yourself so that you can 'see' and experience it in order to know if it is 'right'. Shall I go on a long term mission to a particular country? Try going to this nation for a short length of time and get a feel for it. Which college or university shall I attend next Summer? Try attending an 'Open Day' and find out what it's really like. God's full will is rarely displayed through an atlas or through a prospectus. These may act as bait, but 'seeing' something for yourself, will reel it in! Guidance is often easier than we make it.

20th July

"How can I be sure?" (Lk. 1:18)

"I am the Lord's servant" (Lk. 1:38)

In one of the longest chapters to be found in the New Testament, we see some similarities between the experiences of Zachariah and Mary. Both:

- were visited by an angel (v11, v28)
- were afraid (v12, v30)
- were promised sons who would be 'great' (v15, v32)
- responded with a question (v18, v34)

However, there was one marked difference between the two, Zachariah expressed **doubt** whereas Mary expressed **devotion**. Zachariah became mute, Mary sang 'The Magnificat'.

If the Lord tells us to do something seemingly impossible, don't ask, 'How can I be sure?' rather respond, 'I am the Lord's servant'.

21st July

'The Israelites sampled their provisions but did not inquire of the Lord.' (Josh. 9:14)

When deciding on making an unholy alliance, God's people relied solely on what they could see not on the One who sees what cannot be seen naturally.

There's certainly a place to use common sense but only alongside consulting the Spirit.

In decision-making we use our intelligence and we inquire of the Lord.

22nd July

'This amazed everyone and they praised God, saying, 'We have never seen anything like this.''   (Mk 2:12)

In Mark's Gospel we see the authority of Jesus.

Mark 1 - Lord over **Sickness**
Mark 2 - Lord over **Sin**
Mark 3 - Lord over the **Sabbath**
Mark 4 - Lord over **Storms**
Mark 5 - Lord over **Satan**

What do you need His power over today? He is more than enough!

23rd July

"Did God really say..?" (Gen. 3:1)

The serpent didn't tempt Adam and Eve to steal, murder or commit adultery but to simply question what God had already said. He knows that if we fall for the latter, the former will soon follow.

24th July

'As iron sharpens iron, so one person sharpens another...' (Prov. 27:17)

When metal rubs against metal, inevitably sparks will fly! Rough edges do not always smooth out easily and quickly. Patience and persistence is needed aplenty.
As with the natural, so with the spiritual. Inevitably as leaders and personalities interact, tensions can run high at times and disagreements can soon follow. However, if we want to enjoy the sharpening, we have to endure the sparks. The process is as important as the end product.

25th July

'My prayer...is that all of them may be one...' (Jn 17:20-21)

Jesus' desire, not in a 'preach' nor parable but in a prayer, was that his Church may be unified. Unity does not mean conformity but it does mean concord. We are different, but our diversity does not cancel out our unity - it celebrates it!

26th July

'Everyone should be quick to listen, slow to speak' (Jam. 1:19)

We live in a world where we believe we deserve to be heard. We have our opinions and we want them to be made known above everyone else's. What I learn from the private interactions of Jesus with people from all walks of life is that not only did He speak, but at times He was silent – to listen (Lk. 24:17-19).

The word SILENT and LISTEN are both spelt with the same letters – think about that! We have been given two ears and one mouth – perhaps we should listen twice as much as speak.

Who around you today needs a listening ear?

27th July

As a writer, I produce many social media posts. Looking back over some old posts, it could seem to some that my life is successful, action-packed and very exciting. Although I am grateful for what I have been privileged to see, achieve and do so far, I have also been very careful to highlight the good bits for my 'Friends' to see. What about the wilderness times? What about the times of waiting and wondering? What about the times when I've just had to decide to get out of bed, put one foot in front of another and do what needs to be done that day? These times are certainly not 'Instagram' or 'Kodak' moments. They are purposely omitted and do not make the social media pages or the final cut.

When we read chapters of the Bible, especially in one sitting, we can soon gain the unrealistic picture that the saints of old had action-packed lives where miracles occurred every day and God always spoke and directed them clearly. How untrue! When supernatural events happen too often they cease to be super and special in our minds. Familiarity does breed contempt! Don't forget that after his conversion, Paul spent 3 years in Arabia and Damascus - a time-period covered by only one verse (Gal. 1:18). What did he do during these silent years? We can only guess and fill in the gap. Between the pit and palace experiences - with Potiphar's wife and the prison in between - there are at least 17 years of waiting and wondering for the young Joseph. Had he dropped the ball somewhere? Had he peaked too soon? Was his dream really from God or the result of what he had eaten the night before? The 30-year period between the manger and Christ's ministry is only mentioned in a few verses by Dr Luke and remember that the Book of Acts (or Action) does cover a 30-year period too and gives the main highlights of the Early Church. What did the believers do in between? Faithfully serve Jesus in the midst of growing persecution.

If most days seem a little 'hum-drum' and 'unspiritual' because the dead have not been raised, prayers don't appear to have been answered, audible voices are not heard and the miraculous provision has not yet arrived through the post - don't think you've missed it. Don't let yourself believe you must be out of God's will and don't fall for the lie that you are the odd one out. I'm convinced that if Paul, Joseph and Jesus were on social media back in the day, there would be many days when they would have very little to post.

28th July

"Where you go I will go, and where you stay I will stay. Your people will be my people and your God my God." (Ruth 1:16)

If the Book of Ruth teaches us anything it is how God can create a blessed ending out of a difficult start.

The Lord will eventually reward true loyalty, integrity and hard work.

29th July

'When kings went off to battle...David remained in Jerusalem.' (2 *Sam. 11:1*)

If David was a king why did he not go to war with the other kings? Unfortunately, because David stayed, he then strayed!

Ensure you're in the right place at the right time. Not being in the 'battle' opens you up to the 'Bathshebas' around you.

30th July

'Rule over the fish in the sea and the birds in the sky and over every living creature...' (*Gen. 1:28*)

A popular Christian radio station was recently discussing the positive effects on environmental issues that a new presidency in the USA could bring. Although my mind raced to the possible negative effects, it did cause me to think about 'green issues'. It's clear from Scripture that before sin and the Fall, mankind was given responsibility to take care of God's creation (Gen. 1:28; 2:15). As stewards, an account to the Master will one day be given on how we have dealt with what is entrusted to us. However, such an account is a private affair - no steward will be judged on how someone else has performed. Our individual attitude to the environment is therefore a private concern and we each need to act according to our conscience. Interestingly, the Bible seems to have little to say about 'green issues' after sin entered the world - there seems to be more pressing needs than saving a physical world that is being ravaged by such sin and is due for renewal and regeneration after Christ returns. The spiritual seems to have overtaken the physical.

As disciples of Christ caring for our environment in any way we can is still a responsibility but not our first priority. Saving people not saving the planet! I hope the latter doesn't prove to be a distraction from the former.

31st July

'Then I prayed to the God of Heaven and answered the king...' (Neh. 2:4)

For true success, before having key conversations on a horizontal level, remember to have the vertical one first!

AUGUST

1st August

'And God placed in the church...gifts of administration...' (1 Cor. 12:28)

When we think of 'administration' images of piles of paper, filing cabinets and endless 'to do' lists often come to mind. Important and vital though this may be in the successful running of any organisation, the Apostle Paul had a different idea in mind.

The word 'administration' in Greek is a word very seldom used in the New Testament - a form is found in Acts 27, Paul's journey and subsequent shipwreck en route to Rome, and in verse 11 it is translated 'pilot' and can literally mean 'to steer' or 'to navigate'.

How imperative it is for any leadership team to ensure those with this often misunderstood gift are part of the crew. The ability to steer a group of people through sometimes difficult waters, to navigate from A to B through often unknown territory, to enable all on board to keep their heads above the waves is not a luxury, but a necessity.

When the waters rage, it is not the MC with the microphone in the ballroom that is needed, but the one with the compass in the cockpit.

2nd August

"Look up at the stars...so shall your offspring be." (Gen. 15:5)

After God gave a word to Abram, there then followed the more difficult stage of waiting.

Process will always follow a promise! Trusting takes time. Rushing the fulfilment will ruin the result.

3rd August

'When I heard these things, I sat down and wept. For some days I mourned and fasted and prayed before the God of heaven.' (Neh. 1:4)

Before God can do a work through us He has to do a work in us. We have to be truly moved in our hearts before we can start to move our hands.

4th August

THAT EUREKA MOMENT!

'Philip found Nathaniel and told him, 'We have found the One..." (Jn 1:45)

When Philip, himself, found Christ he then went to find someone else to tell them about his discovery. The **found** became the **finder!**

Interestingly, the word 'find' or 'found' is used at least five times in John 1 and is the transliteration - 'EUREKA'. It is a statement of immense joy and revelation, arguably the same word used by both the ancient mathematician Archimedes and the gold miners of California in 1849. In fact, Eureka" remains the State motto for California to this day.

When you have a revelation, make it information. Pass on your 'Eureka!' moment. In Christ we have made the most important discovery known to man. Find someone and tell them. The found needs to become the finder!

5th August

'For God so loved the world that he gave....' (John 3:16)

A 'so' should always be followed by a 'that'. True love is never contained within but becomes the ultimate motivator to act out.

However, as Christ-followers, our **motivation** should never be confused with our **message**. Love is not the full message of the Gospel. There are vital and sometimes unpopular components such as sin, separation, salvation and sanctification that need to be communicated to a lost world - but love is the full motivation to share the full message.

In not one of the clear examples of Gospel-preaching in the Book of Acts is the subject of 'love' mentioned by the apostles and evangelists - plenty about the birth, life, death, resurrection, ascension and return of Christ. Are the apostles therefore without love? Absolutely not! When talking about his ministry of persuasion Paul states, 'the love of Christ compels me....' (2 Cor. 5:14) In 1 Corinthians 13, to the same Church, the same apostle writes eloquently about the necessity of love, a chapter surrounded by two long chapters on spiritual gifts!

To fulfil our ministry today, the church needs to be fuelled by love and then show love in action to both the world and each other. However, to preach a 'Gospel of Love' only is to sell people short. Love is the motivator, Christ is always the message!

6th August

From Joshua Chapter 1, if the people of God were going to stand any chance of taking what the Lord had for them, they needed to:

- Forget the **Past** (v2) - history is to be learned from, not lived in.
- Begin to **Prepare** (v2) - failing to prepare is preparing to fail.
- Know His **Promise** (v3) - the promise sees us through the predicament.
- Understand the **Parameters** (v4) - God is often in the detail.
- Obey His **Precepts** (v8) - God tells us what to do and how to do it.
- Experience His **Presence** (v9) - Every time in Scripture when God tells His people to do something significant, He always promises His presence.

Don't just enter what God has for you, possess it!

7th August

'When the wicked rule, the people groan.' (Prov. 29:2)

The Scriptures seem to have little to say about electing earthly authorities. In the Old Testament, the people rejected their

Heavenly King to choose an earthly king with almost immediate disastrous results and by New Testament times, Rome had ceased to be a republic and was now an empire where even the Senate was an unelected body by the ordinary people of the day. Interestingly, in both eras, God allowed both systems of human governance - democracy and dictatorship and although God 'allowing' and God 'wanting' are not necessarily synonymous, his advice to His people was clear - 'pray for those in authority' (1 Tim. 2:1ff) and 'be obedient and loyal subjects' (Rom.13:1ff) unless the essence of the Christian faith is compromised (Acts 5:29). If we are part of a democratic country we should certainly use the vote bought by the sacrifice of others - God can cope with democracy and He gives free will for us to make choices. However, with free will comes responsibility and consequences, good or bad. The Israelites were quick to choose a personality who looked the part and would put them on the world stage with other nations instead of choosing one with integrity of heart. Godly policies usually follow from a godly person and although Scripture is silent on voting, principles on what is close to God's heart is loud and clear, including 'speaking for those who can't speak for themselves, the rights of all who are destitute.' (Prov. 31:8)

When we vote in local or general elections, time will tell if the right people are elected to power. But this is certain, any policy of man that is contrary to God's precepts and principles will ultimately fail and judgment will come. Whilst we wait, we should pray for our rulers, we should declare God's unshakable and everlasting Kingdom like never before and live in the light of Christ's soon return when He alone will reign in truth and righteousness for eternity.

8th August

'We instructed you how to live in order to please God, as in fact you are living.' (1 Thess. 4:1)

Naturally speaking, when you truly love someone you want to do those things that please that person. As with the natural, so with the spiritual. If as Christ-followers we truly love our Lord and Master, we will naturally want to do those things that please Him. What are such things:

- Living by faith (Heb. 11:6)
- Praying for others (1 Tim. 2:1-3)
- Living by the Spirit (Rom. 8:8)
- Doing good and sharing (Heb. 13:16)
- Integrity (1 Chron. 29:17)
- Fearing the Lord (Ps. 147:11)
- Praising the Lord (Ps. 69:30-31)

Pleasing God is not just an attitude, it has to be an action.

9th August

'But now that you have been set free from sin and have become slaves of God, the fruit you get leads to sanctification and its end, eternal life.' (Rom. 6:22)

Moses led Israel out of **bondage**, but it was Joshua who took them into **blessing**. Moses brought them through the Red Sea, but Joshua took them over the Jordan River. Moses led the people out, but Joshua led them in. Moses is the symbol of deliverance, but Joshua the emblem of victory.

In the Christ life, the 'Moses' stage of salvation has to take place before the 'Joshua' stage of sanctification can take over. It's not enough to be redeemed **from** the world, we need to be victorious **over** the world!

When we decide to follow Christ, it's just the beginning!

10th August

'What is crooked cannot be made straight...' (Eccl. 1:15)

It is difficult not to be disturbed by current events. Confusion

reigns! However, one thing is clear, something 'crooked' has invaded our world and as the Scripture writer investigated and discovered some 3000 years ago, no amount of education (Eccl. 1:13), pleasure (Eccl. 2:1), alcohol (2:3), achievements (2:4), possessions (2:7), wealth (2:8) or fame (2:9) will straighten it.
The hope for our world today is not in a new government or new policies - believing such is like 'chasing the wind'. As the writer eventually discovered at the end of his long and somewhat depressing quest, the answer is always higher than us - 'Remember your Creator' (Eccl. 12:1.

In the final analysis, all that is 'crooked will fall' (Prov. 28:18) and a day of judgement awaits all. Truth always prevails. Though it may see that 'confusion reigns' - in fact, the Lord reigns. He always has and always will. He can never be voted out of office, He will not abdicate His throne. He alone will make crooked paths straight in His way and in His time. Our task is to simply trust!

11th August

'We are not like Moses, who would put a veil over his face to prevent the Israelites from seeing the end of what was passing away.' (2 Cor. 3:13)

It would seem there were two reasons Moses wore a veil - initially, to shield the people from the powerful glory of God, but then to shield them from the truth and reality when the same glory started to fade.

As church leaders, there is a real temptation to keep up a pretence, to continue to wear a secular 'veil' when the spiritual glory departs. If we are honest, we don't adjust so much to protect our sheep but, if the truth be known, to protect ourselves as shepherds. This new 'veil' comes in all shapes and sizes - new programmes, shorter and snappier church services, a change in name, personnel, decor, worship style, dress....even fancy coffee and muffins. There may well be a place to shake things up, but be careful we are not continuing to wear a veil of our own doing to fool others, and especially ourselves, that all is well.

There is no substitute for the authentic, manifest glory of God in our gatherings.

12th August
"It would take more than half a year's wages to buy enough bread for each one to have a bit!" (Jn. 6:7)

Every miracle in the Bible started off as a problem! If you have a problem today then there is potential for God to move on your behalf. If there is a mountain in your way, then there is a miracle on its way!

13th August
'And all of Israel could see that Samuel was a prophet of the Lord.' (1 Sam. 3:20)

If you have a gift, you don't need to **publicise** it because others will **recognise** it! What are your gifts, be they natural or supernatural? If you are yet to discover your ministry and place in the body of Christ try these for size:

Delve – look around and ask, 'Where are the **gaps** in the local church? What needs to be done?'
Do – speak to your leadership and have a **go** at one or more of these ministries for a set period of time.
Discern – after a while ask **God,** yourself and others, 'Where is there fruit? What do I enjoy?'
Develop – **Grow** in this area of ministry by getting alongside others, reading or taking a course.
Find your place and function!

14th August
'And who knows but that you have come to your royal position for such a time as this?' (Est. 4:14)

'Who knows?' - God knew!

At the beginning of the story of Esther, throughout the first five chapters, the statement can be rightly made - 'God is nowhere!' His name is not mentioned throughout the ten chapters of this book, the queen is removed, a replacement is found though she hides her true identity, a plot is hatched to kill the king, Haman vowed a genocide against all 75,000 plus Jews in Persia at the time and he built a gallows to hang the righteous Mordecai, cousin and guardian of the new queen.

I'm so glad that this book does not end at Chapter 5.

The first five chapters may state 'God is nowhere' but the second five chapters stress that 'God is now here!' Esther was in the right place at the right time to protect her people, the king was saved, Mordecai's good deeds were rewarded and the evil Haman was hung on his own gallows.

Perhaps you are in the middle of your story right now and it appears that 'God is nowhere!' Realise that another five chapters are coming and your story is not finished. At the end, may you come to realise the providence and faithfulness of a God who is always working in the background on your behalf and will soon reveal himself as the God who is 'now here!'

15th August

'Mary sat listening at Jesus' feet whilst Martha became distracted by the work that needed to be done...' (Lk. 10:39-40)

Somehow we need to keep a Mary spirit in a Martha society - to find a way of worship in the midst of a world of work.

16th August

''Leave her alone' Jesus replied....' (Jn. 12:7)

After Jesus publicly rebuked Judas for his attitude and words, the next time he is mentioned, the devil had already prompted him to betray the Lord. Perhaps, in a strange way, the betrayer himself felt betrayed by Christ.

My friend, if you come under discipline, be it public or private, be careful to take it and even thank God for it. Don't get bitter but always better. Never let it drive a wedge between you and others...the consequences for all are always disastrous.

Remember, the Lord punishes His enemies but He disciplines those He loves. Discipline is a part of discipleship.

17th August

The One who is building His Church, still speaks to His Church - not only the Church **global**, but especially the Church **local**. In Revelation 2 and 3 the same Jesus had something to say to 7 local churches in Asia Minor. Each message was not prophetic of some End Time event, but it was unique and relevant to what they were going through at that particular time - a commendation and a complaint!

Church leader today, realise that the Lord is as aware of your present as He is of your future. He wants to speak into your situation as He is well acquainted with your struggles and successes. 'He who has an ear, let him hear'.

18th August

'They that wait upon the Lord shall renew their strength...' (Is. 40:31)

I hate waiting rooms - be they at the dentist or the doctor. I would much rather walk from the street into the surgery at my allocated appointment time, but often they are running over and I have to endure this place in between containing old copies of magazines and people making nervous conversation. The sound of the dentist's drill in the next room doesn't help.

God often has a 'waiting room' - a place in-between what we have been doing and what He now wants us to do. Unfortunately, we can't always go straight from one to another, there is often a season of waiting, preparing, refining and trusting. Such places can either be endured or enjoyed - the choice is ours.

It's in the waiting! However, the waiting doesn't have to be a time of stress unless we let it. The Prophet Isaiah tells us it should be a time to gain strength - strength for the next leg of the Christian race.

19th August

'I planted the seed, Apollos watered it, but God makes it grow.' (1 Cor. 3:6)

We live in a world where immediate, visible results are expected. Ask any Premier League football manager. Success is in the seen! In God's economy it is so different as much of what we do is unseen by other people and off their radar - a spiritual 'seed' is planted in the soil and hidden, the same 'seed' is watered with Scripture and the Spirit which soaks down into the 'earth' seemingly lost. However, in time, God fulfills His part of the process and when the conditions are right, a seedling springs up and all is well.

Take heart today! If your role involves being out of the limelight, appears irrelevant and unneeded, then remember this - before the fruit is seen, faithfulness in the unseen has to take place.

20th August

'My grace is sufficient for you...' (2 Cor. 12:9)

God's grace is not always getting Heaven's blessings, but being kept through the world's burdens. We are not only saved by grace in the past, but we are being sustained by grace in the present.

21st August

'They made me take care of their vineyards, but my own vineyard I have neglected.' (Song of Sol. 1:6)

How easy to bear fruit away from home yet forget about the 'vines' closest to us.
Those entrusted to us are not a distraction from the ministry, they are our ministry!

22nd August

'Jesus wept.' (Jn 11:35)

The shortest verse in the entire Bible with a long, deep meaning. Although the Lord knew that resurrection for Lazarus was just around the corner and that the sisters' mourning would soon turn to dancing - because they wept, He wept.

Despite your current circumstances dictating otherwise, do not let yourself be told that God is distant, cold, heartless and uninterested in your tears. Psalm 56:8 states that the God of the Universe stores them 'in bottles'. Whether this is to be taken literally or not, the Lord is always aware and takes account of what affects us. Even though a 'resurrection' may well be in your near future, because you weep in the present, He does too.

He is touched when you are touched. What moves you, moves Him.

23rd August

'But the men said, '....these people are stronger than we are." (Num. 13:31)

Even though all twelve saw the same territory, ten said 'No' but two said 'Go!' Ten saw the **giants** but two looked beyond the problem to view the potential- they saw the **grapes**.

The majority are not always correct in God's economy. We all remember the names of the positive two, very few today remember any of the names of the negative ten.

24th August

'How long will you waver between two opinions? If the Lord is God, serve him - If Ba'al is God, serve him.' (1 Kings 18:21)

There's a story told that during the US Civil War, a man who lived on the Mason-Dixon Line couldn't decide which side to fight for - the North or the South. He decided to fight for both and carried a flag pole bearing both the Union and Confederate flags, one on each side. The result? He was shot by both sides!

You can't have a foot in two camps. You can't serve two masters! Christ is either Lord of all or He's not Lord at all.

25th August

'Here I am! I stand at the door and knock. If anyone hears my voice and opens the door, I will come in...' (Rev. 3:20)

Although this is a text used in gospel presentations and often to great effect, the context shows that the invitation was actually given to lukewarm believers in a local church in modern-day Turkey.

Know today that the same Jesus won't 'gatecrash' your life, but He waits for the invitation to enter every room of your being and to stoke the fireplace in each. Remember, the handle to your heart is always on the inside!

26th August

In Acts 15, a great controversy arose that threatened the Early Church in its infancy. We are told that Paul and Barnabas were brought into 'sharp dispute' (v2) with others. However, in the midst of something that could have aggravated the Church at that time, they managed to reach some sort of agreement. How was this done?

-There was a place for **discussion** and **debate** (v9);

-There was a place for **diversity**. We are told that the 'apostles' were present but also some
elders, or local leaders, were there too (v6). We are told that various characters were able to
speak (Peter, Barnabas, Paul and James etc);

-There was a place for biblical **discovery** - what did the Scriptures say on this issue? (v16-18);

-There was a place for Holy Spirit **direction** (v28).

In the pursuit of unity and the 'mind of the Lord', let there be a place for all of these.

27th August

'Do not put out the Spirit's fire.' (1 Thess. 5:19)

In God's kingdom, it's always cool to be hot!

28th August

I HAVE A DREAM!

On the 28th August, 1963 Dr Martin Luther-King gave his now famous speech from the steps of the Lincoln Memorial. Although he was one of 18 speakers that day, his words will be the ones people remember for years to come.

Similarly, Joseph of old had a dream (Gen. 37:5). We can learn the following:

-His dream **came to pass**, but not immediately (Gen. 47:12);

Often the dream is tested through the pit and prison before the full reality in the palace.

-Be careful who you **share** your dream with (Gen. 37:5);

The 'brothers' around you will either seek to destroy your dream or develop it.

-Make sure your dream is **from the Lord**

Time will tell whether your dream is a God-thing or just a good-thing!

29th August

According to Nehemiah 3:1, the first gate to be repaired by the returning exiles was the Sheep Gate. The unblemished lambs would pass through this gate to be offered in sacrifice and worship to a Holy God.

Everything we do as follows of Christ stems from His ultimate sacrifice for us. We serve from a place of position with the Lord and not point-scoring for the Lord. When this 'gate' is built first and standing strong in our lives all the other 'gates' will follow.

30th August

Nehemiah 3:6 states that the Old Gate was repaired along with the others.

In the midst of the fresh and the new, there is always a place for the old to be rebuilt, repaired and remembered.

We reject and deny centuries' old traditions at our peril.

31st August

'Take some of the blood and place it on the right ear of the Priest, the right thumb and on the big toe of his right foot...then take some of the anointing oil and sprinkle it on his garments...' (Ex. 29:20-21)

Anointing with oil can only follow cleansing by blood. As 'priests' of our God make sure that today, and every day, what we hear (ears), what we do (hands) and where we go (feet) are under the covering of His blood and control of His Spirit.

SEPTEMBER

1st September

'The tongue also is a fire...' (Jam. 3:6)

Together with her brother Richard, Karen Carpenter formed the singing sensation, The Carpenters. During a 14-year period they sold close to 90 million albums, toured the world and won many awards. In Time magazine, Karen was named in the top 100 most influential singers of all time and had a voice that felt she was singing just to you. At the height of their fame, a journalist described the young duo as, 'the talented Richard and his chubby younger sister, Karen.' On reading such words she began to see herself in a different light, started dieting and developed anorexia. Despite hospital treatment it was too late - she died as skin and bone of heart failure at the tender age of just 32.

Let's watch our words. Forest fires often start due to negligent actions, without thinking or caring. Similarly, damage is done in people's lives by throw-away words, even in so-called 'jest'. Once the arrow is fired from the bow it's on its way to the target - it can't be taken back.

If we can't say anything encouraging and constructive - let's say nothing at all. 'Kill' the world with kindness.

2nd 'September

'Let him who is without sin...' (Jn 8:7)

This is a verse I've heard quoted much over the years - mostly, in my humble opinion, out of context. To say that no one can make and pass judgement on someone because no one is perfect is clearly illogical and also not what Jesus had in mind on this occasion. If no one can call out wrong, if no one is held to account then the judges can't pass a sentence, the police cannot bring law and order, parents can't discipline, teachers can't bring a level of decorum. Believe me, we don't want to live in a world like this where there are no enforcers of the rules because we're imperfect ourselves. The best games of football as a kid were always those with a referee!

Jesus has something specific in mind on the occasion of a woman taken in adultery. The Pharisees are clearly the focus of His attention and words. They were inconsistent with God's law, often twisting it to suit their own cause and means. The law stated that both the man and woman caught in the immoral act were to be punished. Where was the man? Why wasn't he called out? They had it in for the woman only and were therefore unfair and inconsistent in their attitude and actions.

Even though none of us wish to do it, there is actually a time and a place to judge as Christ-followers. 1 Corinthians 5:12-13 sees Paul commanding it in a certain context and Jesus expects us to look for fruit. There is a place to call out right and wrong, though the lines continue to become blurred in our post-modern world. There's a right way to judge and a wrong way. Be fair, be biblical, be consistent, be firm, be gracious. If you are guilty of the same issue then you can't bring the charge - that's the 'plank in your own eye'. Let others act. Where there is genuine remorse and repentance there is always restoration and a re-start.

3rd September

'For three years now I've been coming to look for fruit on this fig tree but haven't found any. Why should it use up soil? Cut it down...' (Luke 13:7)

In the Lord's 'vineyard' everything we grow for God is to be tested with time. If no fruit is displayed then there comes a point when precious 'soil' or resources should not be used up but rather what we are attempting to do needs to be dug up - in order to make space for something else.

Much of what we grow is **good**...but not always of **God**. The important factor is to both acknowledge and accept the difference.

4th September

The Optimist says: 'My cup is half full'

The Pessimist says: 'My cup is half empty'

The Psalmist says: 'My cup overflows!'

He is the God of the plenty! May He be so for you today!

5th September

'The Lord came down to see the tower they were building...' (Gen. 11:5)

'They looked for a city whose builder and architect is God.' (Heb. 11:10)

Towers built to man's plans will cause total **confusion**, but cities built to His design will lead to true **contentment.**

In your dreams and desires, make sure God is the Initiator and not just the Inspector!

6th September

'Sing o barren woman...break into song..' (Is. 54:1)

Anyone can sing when their team is winning, much harder when the chips are down. However, the prophet is commanding not the fruitful nation of Israel to sing, but the barren one. The true song of faith comes before conception, not during pregnancy or birth.

Today, do not underestimate the power of singing in the storm. If Jesus could sing before Calvary (Matt. 26:30), if Paul could sing in confinement (Acts 16:25), if the exiles could sing in captivity (Ps. 137:3) - what's our excuse?

7th September

'You also, like living stones, are being built into a spiritual house...' (1 Pet. 2:5)

The true Church of Jesus is not made up of dead bricks, but living stones - people not a place.

Bricks are uniform in size, stones are uniquely shaped!

8th September

'So he rebuilt the wall...' (Neh. 4:6)

How often we want new resources, the 'best' people, a blank canvas to build for God. Nehemiah used the same damaged stones to put up a wall to the glory of God.

Rebuilding comes from the rubble. Masterpieces from broken pieces! Use what you have, use who you have! God will be glorified!

9th September

'After he said this, he was taken up before their very eyes, and a cloud hid him from their sight.' (Acts 1:9)

The Ascension of Christ is an oft forgotten doctrine in the Christian Church. The Ascension doesn't mean the loss of His intimacy, leadership and advocacy; it confirms the magnification and availability of them all. Because Christ's ascended:

-He has Sent His Spirit (Jn 15:26)

-He is Preparing a Place (Jn 14:2)

-He is Acting as our Advocate (1 Jn 2:1)

-He is Praying for His People (Heb. 7:25)

-He is Coming with, and for, His Church (1 Thess. 4:16-17)

Christ has died, Christ has risen, Christ will come again!

10th September

'To the first servant he gave five talents, to the second he gave two talents and to the third servant, one...' (Matt. 25:15)

It's never the number of talents the Master gives His servants that counts, it's what we do with what He has given us that brings the reward. Attitude and action over amount every time.

Be labourus, not lazy with the time, talents and treasure He has entrusted to you. Don't look over the fence, focus on your own 'garden'.

11th September

'Taste and see that the Lord is good; blessed is the one who takes refuge in him.' (Ps. 34:8)

In days like these we can feel unsafe and uncertain, with many questions in our mind - what will happen to my job, my health, my family, my future? Such worries come as we feel out of control of the circumstances and therefore we fear the consequences.

We can seek to allay such anxieties through others, through our bank accounts or through bunkering down in the safety of our homes. When we take refuge in something physical, we are trusting it will take care of us or at least make us feel safe and secure. When we take refuge in God, we are offering that trust to Him instead. We are finding a place of calm in the eye of the storm through trusting not trying - though the tornado still rages around.

In 1763, the Rev. Augustus Toplady was making his way home from 'Evensong' when he was caught in a sudden storm in Burrington Combe on the Mendip Hills. Finding shelter in a gap in the gorge, he was struck by his experience and later scribbled down the initial lyrics to the timeless hymn:

'Rock of ages, cleft for me, let me hide myself in Thee'.

Whatever your storm, God may not take you out of it, but He's promised to see you through it.

12th September

'Forgetting the past and looking forward to what lies ahead, I press on to reach the end of the race..' (Phil. 3:13-14)

The Christian race is not a short sprint, but a long steeplechase - there are many obstacles to overcome and often we will hit hurdles and stumble. However, when this happens, the best athletes forget about the last hurdle and focus on the next. Dwelling on the disappointments of the past will greatly distort our preparation for what lies ahead. Although history should always be learned from, it should never be lived in - what's happened, has happened - a new challenge awaits.

Those things we come across in the lane of life are never walls to stop us but merely obstacles to spur us on. We are called to be 'overcomers' (1 Jn 4:4). However we can only be an 'overcomer' if we have something to overcome!

13th September

FIFTEEN TO ONE!

I am reminded again of the Apostle Paul's instructions to Timothy on how and who to choose for leadership roles in God's Kingdom (1 Tim. 3:1-7). Interestingly, there seems to be 15 personal character traits to look for and yet only 1 concerning our public platform abilities - 'must be able to teach'. Please do not get me wrong, the Church certainly needs not only those with a gift but those who are a gift to the Body of Christ - Ephesians 4:11 is very clear about that. However, how quick we are to choose gift over godliness or charismata over character. When Jesus gave a visual aid of true service, he took the towel and not the microphone!

Our world is quick to choose those who can perform and 'do' but not always those who 'are'. Qualifications and work experience are always at the top of any CV or Application Form.
Like Joseph, we should be people of integrity and innovation. Samson, on the other hand, seemed to have the power, yet lacked purity. I know who I'd rather model.

May our gifting never take us where our character can't keep us.

14th September

'James, Peter and John, those esteemed as pillars...' (Gal. 2:9)

The Church today doesn't need pew-fillers, it needs pillars. Pillars are solid, upright, straight - they bear the building, the building doesn't bear them. They are permanent fixtures who stand on a firm foundation.

15th September

'Wanting to satisfy the crowd, Pilate released Barabbas to them and had Jesus flogged..' (Mark 15:15)

When under pressure, like Pilate, do we default to pleasing people or appeasing the Almighty? We can either satisfy those around or the One above. We can do the popular thing or the right thing - rarely both at the same time.

16th September

'It is not for you to know the times or dates the Father has set...But you will receive power when the Holy Spirit comes on you; and you will be my witnesses...' (Acts 1:7-8)

With every Christian doctrine there are clear extremes and the teaching of the End Times, or Eschatology, is no different. Both extremes are unhelpful and unhealthy. On one hand there are committed and sincere believers who spend countless hours determining, without doubt, the exact order of events and the meaning of every symbol given in Revelation. Some have historically gone as far as 'date-setting' and selling their property to prepare for the Parousia, only to be left feeling embarrassed with 'eschatological egg' on their faces. This is folly! Such 'teaching' sadly plays on people's fears - it produces quite a following and sells merchandise.

The other extreme is equally as bad. Many in church life today are sadly ignorant of even the basics of Christ's Return and the main events surrounding it. This is foolish! This is surprisingly true in contemporary Pentecostal circles - whereas our spiritual forefathers were nicknamed 'the Second Comers' as a sermon and a song on such a subject were part of the staple diet of most meetings. I, personally, can't remember the last time I heard a clear, expository message on this subject nor sang a new song about it. Why is this? Perhaps we have become settled and comfortable with life on Earth? Perhaps we don't like to preach on it because we, as preachers, are confused about the details ourselves? It is interesting that in countries and communities where persecution and death is a clear and present danger they long for heaven and Christ's Return more than those of us in relative comfort. The opposed Early Church certainly hoped for His coming with the word 'Maranatha' or 'Come, our Lord' said in unison at the end of their secret gatherings.

As with most beliefs, the answer perhaps lies somewhere in the middle. We can never be 100% certain of the exact details of 'Revelation' - it's apocalyptic writing, strongly symbolic and therefore not literal in the main. We can do our own research, consult the commentators and have our own personal theories on the identity of the 'dragon' with its 'seven heads, ten horns and seven crowns'. We can have our views on whether Christ will return before, during or after the Tribulation and if this takes place before or after the Millennium - or if, in fact, there will be a Millennium.

At the end of the day, all we know for certain is that Christ will return and then everything changes. That's the blessed hope for the born-again. In the meantime, in these apocalyptic days where both believer and unbeliever are searching for a spiritual interpretation to what is and will happen, let's not be distracted by dogmatic details of the End Times nor be ignorant of the basics but allow the knowledge of his coming to fuel our evangelistic efforts like never before. It is not for us to know times or dates, but we have been promised 'power' to witness locally, nationally and internationally.

May His last command be our first priority!

17th September

'I plead with Euodia and I plead with Syntyche to be of the same mind in the Lord.' (Phil. 4:2)

In the church at Philippi, where the gospel was first preached to women (Acts 16:13) and a church first-formed in a woman's home (Acts 16:40), there were two outstanding females. They were 'co-workers' with Paul, had 'contended' for the cause and had their names compiled in the book of life. However, an unknown issue had occurred that caused these saints to fall-out and what possibly started as a private problem had now become public and warranted a response from the founder of the church. Paul pleaded with these sisters to be 'like-minded', 'in harmony' or to 'settle their disagreement' for the sake of the gospel and if need be, receive help from others in the vital reconciliation process.

Inevitably, as believers, we will always disagree on a range of matters both spiritual and secular. We tend to gravitate towards those of similar gifting and genre - and that's ok! We are never commanded to be uniform but we are commanded to be in unity and within such there is always room for much diversity. Although, when 'iron sharpens iron' the inevitable sparks will fly, there is always more to unite us than divide us and such should be sought. A pearl is formed through irritation and gold is purified through heat! That which we don't enjoy is often productive, though painful at the time. However, though we may 'agree to disagree' on various issues, it is never more advantageous to win arguments and lose friends.

To the 'Euodia's' and 'Syntyche's' out there - let's choose to be in harmony though we may be whistling a slightly different tune. In Christ, if in nothing else, there is always more to unite us than divide us.

18th September

'Like an eagle that stirs up its nest and hovers over its young, that spreads its wings to catch them and carries them aloft.' (Deut. 32:11)

A eagle teaching her young eaglets to fly is fascinating. After their birth, the young have everything they need – water, warmth and worms. However, one day, mother eagle will return to the nest and start to stir it up. She then takes one of hers young eaglets and gently throws it over the side of the nest. The eaglet will drop and before hitting the ground, mother eagle will swoop down and catch her young on her back. She will then ascend to the nest and start again. After several attempts, the eaglet will find out that it too has wings and can fly.

Is your comfort zone being stirred right now? Perhaps it's not of the devil but of the Divine! The Lord knows full well that if you want to learn to fly, you need to get out of the nest!

19th September

In James 2 there are three types of faith:

- **Dead** faith (v26)
- **Demonic** faith (v19)
- **Dynamic** faith (v22)

Knowing certain facts is not enough. Even the devil knows Scripture, the right 'Christian' things to say and facts about the sacrificial death of Christ. His demons even 'shake' and show emotion. Such 'faith' is still not enough to save.

For the true believer, living faith needs to prove it is indeed alive by works. There needs to be a vital move from the head, to the heart and through the hands to the world around us. We can never do good works to become right with God - we do good works because we're right with God! Profess, yes! But make sure you practice too!

20th September

'Out of the stump of Jesse's family a shoot will grow...' (Is. 11:1)

Out of nothing can come everything! What appears to be dead in the ground can produce life.

Stumps still produce shoots! Shoots can become Saviours! Does your life seemed barren right now? Blessing is surely on its way!

21st September

'I am the way and the truth and the life. No one comes to the Father except through me.' (Jn. 14:6)

The 'Prince of Preachers' Charles Spurgeon had a strict policy that after he preached he was not to be disturbed in his vestry after the service. On one particular occasion, an old friend of the pastor turned up unannounced to see him. After the service ended, Spurgeon went to his room as usual and his friend asked one of the deacons if he could see the pastor for a few moments as he had travelled a long distance to London. The deacon explained how it was policy that Spurgeon was not to be disturbed and the friend turned to leave the church when he spotted Spurgeon's son. He went to him to explain who he was and asked for special permission to see his father. Spurgeon's son replied, 'Sir, come with me!' They went to the pastor's vestry and knocked on the door. Spurgeon shouted, 'Come in' and looked up. As the door opened, he saw his old friend with his son and exclaimed the words, 'Ah, I see you have come to the father through the son!'

22nd September

'Contend for the faith that was once for all entrusted to God's holy people.' (Jude 3)

In Jude, there is a solemn warning against those who pervert truth and lead others astray. These false teachers:

- Slip in subtly - not invited in (v4);
- Have a distorted view of God's grace (v4);
- Have an incorrect view of the Lordship of Jesus (v4);
- Lack respect for others (v8);
- Are false shepherds (v12);
- Boast about themselves (v16);
- Follow their own instincts and not the Spirit (v19).

However, not only is Jude describing their behaviour in 7 statements, he instructs the believers on how to respond, in 7 statements:

- Realise there is a battle (v3)
- Hold true to truth (v3)
- Be comforted by prophecy (v14-15).
- Build yourselves up in the Faith (v20)
- Pray in the Spirit (v20)
- Stay in God's love (v21)
- Support those who have been led astray (v22)

Sadly, false teachers are still alive and kicking! To be forewarned is to be forearmed!

23rd September

'But the LORD said to my father David, 'You did well to have it in

your heart to build a temple for my Name." (1 Kings 8:18)

King David's overwhelming desire was to build a 'home' for God. However, the task was not to be his but his son, Solomon's. Despite disappointment, David did what he could - he gave of his finance and he gave his unconditional support. The most important factor was not the horizontal praise of men but that the project was completed competently and that the glory went to God - despite the specific vessel used at the time.

You may have had dreams and desires from yesteryear that never came to fruition. You may have discovered that someone else is now 'living your dream!' Don't take a 'dog in the manger' attitude but support them in any way that you can so that the 'temple' is built to the glory of God.

God sees the past and present desires of your heart, every tear is bottled and every cry recorded. As he said to David he will say to you, 'You did well!'

24th September

"Are you all right? Is your husband all right? Is your child all right?' the prophet asked. 'It is well,' she replied...' (2 Kings 4:26)

When the Shunammite woman uttered these words, her child had already passed away in her arms six verses ago.

Faith is declaring that all is well, even though at the time of utterance, all does not appear well.

25th September

'While he was a long way off his father saw him and filled with compassion ran towards him...'
(Lk. 15:20)

As a picture of the Lord, this is the only time in Scripture that we see God running...towards the sinner. I am also led to believe that culturally, not only did a wayward son bring shame upon the family but also on the wider close-knit community. The father here was not only accepting his son privately but protecting his son publicly.

God wants to father you today - to accept you and protect you. He always takes the initiative and runs towards you when we make the vital decision of returning home. Realising, returning, repenting on your part always brings restoration on His part!

26th September

'Who can touch the Lord's anointed?' (1 Sam. 26:9)

Growing up in a Pentecostal/Charismatic setting I often heard this verse quoted and usually meant to mean, 'Don't question or disagree with the man or woman of God!' This often led to little accountability, few parameters and weird and wonderful goings on in the name of Christ. However, a text taken out of context will leave you with a 'con.' When David spoke to his servant he was talking about refraining from slaying King Saul and not physically harming him - not questioning his methods and motives!

In the New Testament we see Paul 'confronting' Peter (Gal. 2:11) and Barnabas had a 'sharp disagreement' with Paul (Acts 15:39). Leaders inevitably disagree but disagreement need not mean disunity. When 'iron sharpens iron' it's inevitable that sparks will fly during the sharpening process. The actions and attitudes of so-called leaders should be questioned by others in a constructive and Christlike manner. We all need the security of the saints. 'Touch not' does not mean 'untouchable'.

In addition, under the New Covenant who are the 'Lord's anointed?' 1 John 2:20 says we all are!

27th September

'But encourage one another daily, as long as it is called 'Today'' (Heb. 3:13)

In the New Testament, the word 'encourage' can be used in two ways:

- To get **behind** someone to spur them on, and

- To come **alongside** someone in order to bring comfort.

No better example is given than from nature. Canadian geese fly in a 'V' formation in order to be stream-lined and preserve energy. They will also 'honk' at the goose in front to spur them on. In addition, if a goose is injured or becomes tired and drops, at least two others will leave the formation, drop with it and stay alongside until it recovers. They will then endeavour to join the rest of the flock later.

Who can you both get behind and come alongside today?

What's good for the goose...

28th September

LESSONS FROM BATTLE (Part 1)

'Do not give up meeting together...' (Heb. 10:25)

On that historic day in 1066, William the Conqueror could not penetrate the strong Saxon army who had banded together to create a wall of defence. To isolate and separate them, he hatched a plan to retreat. When the Saxons saw the Normans running they foolishly ran after them and began to be targeted and picked off one by one by the archers.

Never give up meeting with other believers. Our enemy often seeks to **isolate** before he **invades**.

29th September

LESSONS FROM BATTLE (Part 2)

'He ate and drank and then lay down again...' (1 Kings 19:6)

In mid-afternoon, the famous Battle of Hastings in 1066 saw a stalemate with no side gaining the edge. However, William learned that his enemy were exhausted from a previous battle and long travel and so sought to take advantage by bringing in reinforcements and refreshed soldiers.

Like Elijah, in the midst of battle, **rest** and **refreshment** will help you **refocus**!

30th September

LESSONS FROM BATTLE (Part 3)

'Do not be afraid, I am with you.' (Josh. 1:9)

Whilst the Normans under William were fighting the Saxons

under Harold, a rumour had spread that William had been killed. The Normans began to lose heart until their leader took off his helmet and showed them he was still in the battle alongside them and very much alive. Encouraged, they went on to win!

Today, in the midst of your battle, your Commanding Officer has not deserted you nor died. He stands with you as you face your enemies - so take heart, He is very much alive!

OCTOBER

1st October

'And they laughed at him. But he put them all outside except the child's parents and those who were with him and went in where the child was. Taking her by the hand he said to her, 'Little girl, arise." (Mk 5:40-41)

Not only do we gain faith through God's **word**, but this same faith can either be built or broken by those we allow into our personal **world**.

On one occasion, to perform a resurrection miracle, the Son of God needed to dismiss certain doubters and mockers from His presence and allow a select few to join Him in the miracle room. He didn't need many people around Him, just the right people. Why the choice? Clearly some would help His faith whereas some would hinder His faith.

In the same way that you choose what food and drink you allow into your body each day, you can also choose whom you allow to speak into your life. As Martin Luther supposedly once said, 'I certainly cannot stop the birds from flying in the air, but I can sure stop them from nesting in my hair!'

If Christ was selective on whom he allowed into 'places of privilege', shouldn't we?

2nd October

'They will be called oaks of righteousness, a planting of the Lord...' (Is. 61:3)

Major Oak at Sherwood Forest has been around for centuries. Legend has it that Robin Hood and his fellow outlaws lived amongst its branches or others like it. Interestingly, those who planted such trees from tiny acorns never saw the majesty, or enjoyed the benefits, of what they would one day become.

May we take the time now to sow spiritual 'acorns'. Though we may never sit under the shade of future 'oaks of righteousness' ourselves, the next generations will thank you for them.

Don't live for the moment - leave a legacy!

3rd October

'From the time he put him in charge of his household and of all that he owned, the Lord blessed the household of the Egyptian because of Joseph.' (Gen. 39:5)

God's grace was upon the workplace because God's vessel was there.

We believe in proclamation evangelism but never underestimate the power of your spiritual presence in the secular world. We are called to **be** witnesses (Acts 1:8). Witnessing is being as much as doing!

4th October

''Your servant my husband is dead, and you know that he revered the Lord. But now his creditor is coming to take my two boys as his slaves.' Elisha replied to her, 'How can I help you?" (2 Kings 4:1-2)

'One day Elisha went to Shunem. And a well-to-do woman was there...' (4:8)

In the same chapter, the Lord performs a miracle for both a poor woman and a rich woman. Both had needs.
No matter where someone may be on the economic or social spectrum, all are in need of the same miracle-working God. Today, don't show partiality – pray for all, preach to all, prophesy over all! The Lord doesn't show favourtism, it's forbidden for His followers too (Jam. 2:1).

5th October

'So he ran ahead and climbed a sycamore-fig tree to see him...' (Lk. 19:4)

On this particular day in Jericho, it wasn't so much that Zacchaeus saw Jesus, but that Jesus saw him – even amongst the crowds!

Today, you're not forgotten about nor forsaken. In the midst of many, He still sees you!

6th October

'You are that man!' (2 Sam. 12:7)

When choosing those you allow into your world, always intentionally include a 'Nathan' - those brave enough to say what you **need** to hear, though it may not be what you **want** to hear.
Don't stone those who speak the truth in love, weigh up and submit to what they say. Indeed, their words may save you from disaster down the road.

A 'Nathan' in our life will produce a 'David' - No 'Nathans' usually produces a 'Saul'.

7th October

> *'...and on this law he meditates day and night. He is like a tree planted...'* (Ps. 1:2-3)

When the storms of life come, it's not the size of the shoot that carries you through but the strength of the root. Being planted in God's word and ways brings fruitfulness (Ps. 1:3) and faith (Rom. 10:17).

Today, meditate on His word (Ps. 1:2), memorise His word (Ps. 119:11) and move in response to His word (Jam. 1:22). A blessed day awaits!

8th October

'Whatever you do, do it all for the glory of God.' (1 Cor. 10:31)

The world-famous composer, Johann Sebastian Bach, would always put the initials, SDG, after his compositions - 'Soli-Deo

Gloria' - for God's glory alone!

I wonder whether we can put such initials after every word, thought and deed done today?

9th October

'You yourselves are our letter read of everyone.' (2 Cor. 3:2)

We may not all be **apostles** but we are all **epistles!**

The world may not read the Bible, but they'll certainly read us. What will people read today?

10th October

EMBRACE THE JOURNEY

In the Christian race, God has a tendency to take us on unplanned detours - stop off's that were not on the original itinerary. It was clear that the Apostle Paul was to go to Rome (Acts 27:24) - Caesar had to be stood before, more of the New Testament needed to be written and people waiting to be led to Christ. However, on the way to his destination - a storm and shipwreck caused the crew and passengers to take a detour and end up on the island of Malta for several months. On this island, far from being a waste of time, Paul experienced both miracles (28:9) and material provision (28:7) and in time, continued his journey to his final resting place.

Sometimes we are so caught up with arriving at the destination, we tend to miss the sights and experiences of the journey itself. God is as interested in your present as He is in your future. On our way to God's perfect plan and purpose for our lives, there are often storms and shipwrecks that blow us off course. Conveniently, God has arranged safe havens - islands of both opportunity and favour which are never far away. Such islands are placed to resource and refocus our attention as we continue moving forward.

On your way to 'Rome' you will certainly survive the storm and God has lined-up 'Maltas' for you to enjoy along the way - not endure!

11th October

'And David shepherded them with integrity of heart; with skillful hands he led them.' (Ps. 78:72)

True leadership needs both charisma and character, gifting and grace, ability with the hands and attitude of the heart.

12th October

The Lord is:

-The Good Shepherd (Jn 10:11)

-The Great Shepherd (Heb. 13:20)

-The Chief Shepherd (1 Pet. 5:4)

-My Shepherd (Ps. 23:1)

He will lead and feed, guide and provide...for you today!

13th October

'Preach the word; be prepared in season and out of season...' (2 Tim. 4:2)

Throughout almost 30 years of marriage, my wife has cooked thousands of meals for me. Some I can still remember but most I can't - though I'm convinced they did me good at the time.

Throughout my long Christian walk, I have heard thousands of messages and sermons. Some are still memorable - though most have been forgotten. However, I know they did me good at the time.

Never underestimate the feeding power of the preached Word. It's doing you more good than you realise!

14th October

'...for you are with me, your rod and your staff they comfort me.' (Ps. 23:4)

For the first half of this well-known Psalm, the writer speaks of the Shepherd in the 3rd Person - 'He'. However, from verse 4, when the Psalmist describes the 'valley' and 'enemies,' the Lord is spoken of in the more personal 1st Person - 'You'.

It isn't so much that the Lord has moved any closer to us when we find ourselves in life's valleys than when we were on the mountaintop, but often the dark times are the ones when we perceive His nearness the most.

Although the stars are always in place, it's in the dark sky when we see them more clearly.

15th October

'Hezekiah received the letter from the messengers and read it. Then he went up to the temple of the Lord and spread it out before the Lord. And Hezekiah prayed to the Lord...' (2 Kings 19:14-15)

A troubling letter was sent, out of the blue, to King Hezekiah from the Assyrian king, Sennacherib announcing his evil intentions towards God's people and his disdain for God himself. Assyria had already conquered much of the then known world, including the northern kingdom of Israel, and Jerusalem in Judah certainly did not have the military strength to repel such a powerful force. Hezekiah, the King of Judah did what we all should do when we are faced with problems far bigger than our own human ability to solve them - he went to the Lord. In verse 1, Hezekiah went into the house of the Lord and literally laid out the problem before God. He then sent for the man of God, Isaiah. In this passage we can see a recipe that will help us in times of trouble:

-Go to God first and lay your problems at His feet in prayer;

-Go to God's house;

-Get counsel from God's people.

If trouble comes upon you, out of the blue, pray and lay!

16th October

'He chose David his servant and took him from the sheep pens; from tending the sheep he brought him to be the shepherd of his people Jacob...' (Ps. 78:70-71)

Often the Lord allows us to learn skills in the secular world to be of use in the spiritual world.

Nothing done in faith is ever wasted!

17th October

'Who may stand in his holy place? He who has clean hands and a pure heart...' (Ps. 24:3-4)

I am led to believe there is a certain un-negotiable procedure when in the presence of royalty, for example, you don't turn your back on the Queen, you don't start a conversation with her, you never hold your hand out first.

As with the natural, so with the spiritual.

In an atmosphere of corporate worth-ship to the King of kings, there is a biblical protocol to follow regarding our attitude and actions - we bring ourselves into His **presence** (Ps. 100:4), we approach with **purity** of heart (Ps. 24:3-4), we **practice** swift horizontal reconciliation before offering the vertical gift of praise (Matt. 5:23-24).

If earthly royalty rightly deserves our undivided attention to what is acceptable, how much more our heavenly Majesty?

18th October

'Take up the shield of faith, with which you can extinguish all the flaming arrows of the evil one.' (Eph.6:16)

Whilst under house arrest in Rome with a Roman soldier on guard, Paul wrote the Prison Epistles, including Ephesians. Perhaps, when writing about the full armour of God in chapter 6, he took note of the soldier's armour to illustrate our defence and attack mechanisms available through Christ. The Roman shield was large enough to hide behind. Any body-parts sticking out were in danger of being struck by the enemy's weapons.

There are times when we simply need to hide behind our faith which is well able to protect us from the arrows of despair, discouragement and disappointment.

Be completely covered! Any areas of our lives that are exposed are likely to be hit.

19th October

'Why wasn't this perfume sold for 300 coins?' (Jn 12:5)

'Leave her alone!' (Jn 12:7)

What we say often indicates what's important to us. This single act of devotion by Mary was viewed quite differently by two people present that day:

For Judas, it was a **waste** as he was motivated by exorbitant greed for money. His heart was for financial prosperity and this later became his downfall when he sold Jesus for a tenth of what this perfume was worth.

For Jesus, it was **worship.** His heart was for people, which shows in His hasty defence of Mary's act of extravagant generosity.

Interestingly, after this event in Bethany, both Jesus and Judas were soon to be lifted up - Jesus on a Roman cross, Judas on self-made gallows. For Jesus, He was eventually lifted further - to the right hand of the Father. For Judas, he descended to 'the place where he belongs' (Acts 1:25).

Money or people? The former is to be used and is our servant whilst the latter are to be respected and served. We mix these up at our own peril.

20th October

'And he said to them, 'Follow me, and I will make you fishers of men." (Matt. 4:19)

In evangelism, we may not be able to use a net to catch the multitude but we can certainly go out with a fishing rod to win the individual. Philip the evangelist did both (Acts 8:6 and 8:26-27).

Either way, if we don't cast we won't catch! We are to be 'fishers of men' not keepers of aquariums!

21st October

'Encourage one another daily - whilst it is called 'Today'' (Heb. 3:13)

The English word 'encourage' literally means 'to put something into the heart.' It's been likened to verbal sunshine, not just brightening someone's day but bringing growth and nourishment to the soul.

Look for opportunities to encourage today - like Barnabas, to find a 'John Mark' to get behind and alongside, and see the future potential instead of the current problem.

No one ever died of too much encouragement!

22nd October

'The Lord said, 'If as one people speaking the same language they have begun to do this, then nothing they plan to do will be impossible for them.'' (Gen. 11:6)

Never underestimate the power of ungodly unity. It is something that only God Himself can stop!

If unity without God can build high towers then imagine what godly unison can produce?

23rd October

'I would not have you ignorant...' (1 Cor. 10:1)

On more than one occasion the Apostle Paul forcefully states these words to the Corinthians believers - his desire was for them to be **in** the know, not **out** of it. With the plethora of problems in this local church, not once does Paul attribute any issue to a demon. The antidote was not exorcism, but the exercising of the teaching gift, on this occasion through letter.

Please do not get me wrong, of course the devil exists with his army of darkness - the same apostle to the same church warns us to be 'aware of his schemes' (2 Cor. 2:11). However, every problem in the life of the corporate church, or the individual believer, is not the fault of the demonic. To say, 'The devil made me do it!' is often a cop-out from us taking personal responsibility and gives unnecessary attention to the enemy of our souls.

Many, if not all, of the complex issues of life can be overcome with a correct understanding of what God's Word says about them. However, it needs to move from our head to our hands, in other words, there needs to be a 'doing' that quickly follows the 'hearing'. True belief has to affect our behaviour!

24th October

'The devil said, 'For it is written..." (Matt. 4:5-6)

Don't be fooled! Although he's the Father of Lies, even Satan speaks the truth sometimes.

25th October

'So Christ himself gave some to be...evangelists' (Eph. 4:11)

Phillip was called an Evangelist (Acts 21:8) and the only person in the New Testament given that title. What can evangelists, today, learn from this man:

- He was a **servant** (Acts 6:2-5);
- He was **Spirit-filled** (Acts 6:3-5);
- He **spoke** about Christ (Acts 8:5);
- He **spent** time ministering to individuals (Acts 8:26ff) not just to the crowds (Acts 8:6);
- He ministered in **supernatural** power with **signs** following (Acts 8:7);
- He had **success** with his family (Acts 21:9).

Today, proclaim the Good News through your words, works and way of life!

26th October

'Do this in remembrance of me.' (1 Cor. 11:24)

Before Christ ascended to the Father, He gave His Church two main ordinances or orders – to Baptise and to Break Bread. Both practices have seen changes since our Commanding Officer first gave the orders over 2000 years ago. The second one especially.

There are various names given for the remembrance meal first instituted by the Lord as a Passover meal with disciples – including Breaking of Bread, Communion, Lord's Supper and Eucharist. The practice has also seen an evolution from a simple bring and share meal in the 1st century to liturgical ceremonies in the 21st century. What exactly happens at the table is also debated – is it just a memorial? Is Christ present in the emblems? Is it a means of receiving favour with God or even salvation? Should wine and bread be used or will juice and a cracker suffice?

Whatever our views, according to the Scriptures, we take various looks at the table of the Lord:

-A **backward** look – we remember His body and blood (1 Cor. 11:23-24)

-A **forward** look – we remind ourselves He is coming again (1 Cor. 11:26)

-An **outward** look – we realise each other (1 Cor. 10:17)

-An **inward** look – we reflect on ourselves (1 Cor. 11:28)

The next time you break bread with other believers – remember, remind, realise and reflect.

27th October

'So Christ himself gave some to be...teachers' (Eph. 4:11)

Apollos was a Teacher (Acts 18:25). What can budding teachers learn from this man:

-He was **educated** (Acts 18:24).
Training and gifting often work together.

-He was **eager** to learn from others (Acts 18:27).
Apollos, arguably, became a better teacher because he was willing to become a student.

-He was **encouraged** in his gifting (Acts 18:27) and then became an encouragement to others (Acts 18:27).
The teacher was, himself, taught by a husband and wife teaching team. Notice how Priscilla is named first!

Look for opportunities today to teach God's word. Look for opportunities also to be taught God's word. Teachers should be teachable!

28th October

'What is your life? A vapour that appears for a short while and then vanishes...' (Jam. 4:14)

A small interest of mine is to look at gravestones - it can tell a lot about a person's life - for example, the words engraved by loved ones, the years they were alive, perhaps some of their achievements and whether the grave is still well kept with fresh flowers. I noticed recently, for the first time, that between the date of birth and the date of death there is a dash. The dash represents someone's life. What's my 'dash,' what's your 'dash?' What have we done for God and for our neighbour? Have we been faithful with the talents, treasure and time He has given and will we be able to say with the apostle Paul at the end of each day as well as at the end of our life - 'I have ran the race, I have fought the good fight, I have kept the faith?'

It's important to not only live well, but to die well. Make your 'dash' count!

29th October

'And he brought him to Jesus. Jesus looked at him and said, 'You are Simon ('Reed'), *You will be called Cephas* ('Rock')" *(Jn 1:42)*

Simon was impulsive and in many ways unstable. However, the same Simon, having been reinstated and renewed with God's Spirit, became a stone pillar of the Early Church. Christ named him not for what he was as that time, but for what he would become - by God's grace.

We may see the 'reed' but He sees the 'rock'. We see the problem, He sees the potential.

30th October

'Here I am, I have come to do your will O God!' (Heb. 10:9)

Be careful how you measure success in life. Though many may gage it by the number of employees they oversee, the number of noughts on their salary or even the model and age car they drive - remember, no one was ever heard to say at the end of their life, how they wish they'd spent more time at the office or went on

more overseas holidays! In life there are no dress rehearsals, neither should there be regrets.
Success is relative though it has to be more than living for the moment or living for oneself. For the true Christ-follower it is finding God's purpose for you on His planet and fulfilling the role faithfully until He returns or calls us Home.

Faithfulness to the Lord's call will always lead to fruitfulness - if not in this life, certainly in the next.

31st October

'Do not despise the day of small beginnings...' (Zech. 4:10)

Today is Halloween. This word comes from two words -'Hallows Eve' - which is the day before All Hallows' or All Saints' Day which is on the 1st November. Now you know!

On this day, over 500 years ago, after finally realising that sinful man is made right with a Holy God through **trusting** and not **trying**, Martin Luther nailed his '95 Theses' against the door of the church at Wittenberg University. What began as a local debate of the Church's erroneous teaching of the day soon escalated into what is now known as the Protestant Reformation and has affected and spiritually liberated millions ever since.

Never underestimate your actions. Although seemingly small they can have a massive effect.

NOVEMBER

1st November

'They devoted themselves...' (Acts 2:42)

Interestingly, the first Church did not merely pray, fellowship, accept teaching and break bread.....they were steadfastly loyal and devoted to these important spiritual disciplines in the best and worst of times. The result? 'The Lord added to their number...' (2:47)

True and lasting fruit does not come by merely paying 'lip service' to the Lord's commands but by continued loyalty to the Lord's commands.

Faithfulness leads to fruitfulness!

2nd November

'One person considers one day more sacred than another; another considers every day alike. Each of them should be fully convinced in their own mind.' (Rom. 14:5)

We have just had Halloween, Bonfire Night is around the corner, for our friends from the other side of the 'pond' there is Thanksgiving later this month and then the countdown to Christmas starts. For some of us, it already started 10 months ago.
People ask, Christians in particular, whether it is 'right' to celebrate such festivals. Should children go out 'trick or treating'? Should we really celebrate the antics of a man in 1605 who carried out an act of terrorism? Is 'Thanksgiving' towards God or is it a time just to be thankful for what we have - or both? Should a

Christian put up a Christmas tree with its arguable pagan roots?

It's easy to celebrate a tradition and a time of the year because that's what is done in certain communities and cultures or because we have always done it. Furthermore, we don't want our kids 'missing out' on the fun and being seen to be different. Now that my children have grown up - it's a time to reflect. Over the years, we have tried to follow these criteria:

-Be aware of the original roots of the tradition. In good 'soil' or bad?

-Find a way to celebrate and honour Christ in the tradition. If this can't be done, we haven't celebrated it.

-Use the celebration as a way to witness to others.

I'll leave the last word to the Apostle Paul who offers some good advice with regards to celebrating 'sacred' days:

'...be fully convinced in your own mind'.

3rd November

'I have appointed you as a prophet to the nations.....I will be with you' (Jer. 1:5,19)

'I am calling you to lead my people.....I will be with you' (Josh. 1:2, 9)

'Go and make disciples of all nations...I will be with you' (Matt. 28:19, 20)

Every time God asks His people to do something for Him, He **always** promises His presence!

4th November

'By faith Abel offered to God a better sacrifice than Cain...' (Heb. 11:4)

Two brothers offered sacrifices, one was accepted by God, the other angered God. One was living, the other was lifeless. One was offered in faith, the other was the fruit of one's labour. One was an attitude of the heart, the other was an act of the hands.

As believers under the New Covenant, there are now only two sacrifices that we offer to God:

-Our **Praise** - the fruit of our lips (Heb. 13:15) and;
-Our **Person** - the fruit of our lives (Rom. 12:1).

May such sacrifices be accepted, living, by faith and from the heart.

5th November

'Praise the Lord, my soul, and forget not all his benefits' (Ps. 103:2)

November is a month of remembrance. Today, people in the UK remember Guy Fawkes and friends' failed 'Gunpowder Plot' in 1605 by lighting a bonfire and holding firework displays. On the 11th of this month, the UK and other Commonwealth countries observes Armistice Day when we remember those who made the ultimate sacrifice during the World Wars of the 20th Century plus other wars since. A poppy is worn and a two-minute silence is observed to remember those who lost their lives in conflict. Later this month, on the fourth Thursday, in the USA there is the national holiday of Thanksgiving which began as a day of giving thanks for the blessing of the harvest and of the preceding year.

At this time of national and international remembrance, remember the Lord and forget not all His benefits! Count your blessings, name them one by one and it will surely surprise you what the Lord has done.

6th November

'The Lord has given a command concerning you, Nineveh..' (Nah 1:14)

There is strong evidence that the Prophet Nahum was born and bred in Nineveh, in current day Northern Iraq, and that his ministry and message was mainly for the Ninevites.

Sometimes the Lord calls us to speak to the hardest and most hostile audience of all - our own people - those we know and those who know us. It takes a brave person to survive and thrive in a home town where a 'prophet is often without honour.'

Sometimes our 'going' will involve 'staying!'

7th November

'Now I would not have you ignorant...' (1 Cor. 10:1)

On at least six occasions the Apostle Paul clearly stated to his readers how he wanted them to be in 'the know' regarding certain important subjects:

- Israel's future (Rom. 11:25)

- Israel's past (1 Cor. 10:1)

- Spiritual gifts (1 Cor. 12:1)

- Paul's sufferings (2 Cor. 1:8)

- Satan's schemes (2 Cor. 2:11)

- End time state (1 Thess. 4:13)

Often, what we wish to learn is not what the Spirit and the Scriptures wish to teach us. Which curriculum are we following - the world's or the Word's? Ignorance is not always bliss!

8th November

'Rejoice in the Lord always. I will say it again: Rejoice! Let your gentleness be evident to all. The Lord is near. Do not be anxious about anything but in every situation, by prayer and petition, with thanksgiving, present your requests to God. And the peace of God, which transcends all understanding, will guard your hearts and your minds in Christ Jesus. Finally, whatever is true, noble, right, pure, lovely, admirable, excellent or praiseworthy – think about such things.' (Phil. 4:4-8)

There is an antidote for anxiety:

-**Praise** – Rejoice always (v4)

-**Presence** – Know the Lord is near (v5)

-**Prayer** – Let Him know your needs (v6)

-**Precepts** – Think about His ways and works (v8)

Praising God, knowing His presence, praying to Him and meditating on His precepts will bring peace, that passes all understanding (v7).

9th November

'Champions don't become champions in the ring - they are merely recognised there!' (Unknown)

David's battle with Goliath wasn't won in the public fight before men, but in the private fields before God.

10th November

'You will make known to me the path of life; in Your presence is fullness of joy; in Your ***right hand*** *there are pleasures forever.' (Ps. 16:11)*

'Wondrously show Your lovingkindness, O Saviour of those who take refuge at Your ***right hand*** *from those who rise up against them.' (Ps. 17:7)*

'This Jesus God raised up again, to which we are all witnesses. Therefore, having been exalted to the ***right hand*** *of God, and having received from the Father the promise of the Holy Spirit, He has poured forth this which you both see and hear.' (Acts 2:32-33)*

At God's **right hand** of favour there is **pleasure, protection** and **promise!**

May you experience all three today!

11th November

The well-known saying attributed to Francis of Assisi, 'Go and preach the gospel and if you have to, use words..' is not biblical. The New Testament word for 'preach' such as keryxate, and its associated words, clearly expresses the idea of sounds made by the mouth that can be heard.

Although our works need to back up our words and our lifestyle needs to parallel our lips - one is not a substitute for the other. They cooperate not compete!

In obedience to Acts 1:8, Peter went on to preach in Jerusalem and Judea, Philip preached in Samaria and Paul preached to the uttermost parts of the earth. Their commission is still our mission!

12th November

'The testing of your faith produces perseverance...' (Jam. 1:3)

For anything to become 'fit for purpose' it has to go through a series of tests. An aeroplane engine has to be put through its paces before it can be trusted to be airborne with precious lives onboard. As with the natural, so with the spiritual. Any nobody who became somebody in God's Word had times of testing to prove themselves 'fit for Kingdom purpose'.

God will never tempt you to fail and fall but He will always test you in order for you to flourish. Before He trusts you with his Kingdom and precious lives He will usually test you first. Don't be surprised if it happens but be concerned if it doesn't happen!

13th November

'Go to the lake and throw out your line. Take the first fish you catch; open its mouth and you will find a four-drachma coin. Take it and give it to them for my tax and yours.' (Matt. 17:27)

The Lord still has a wonderful way of providing exactly what is needed at exactly the right time...but not exactly in the way we expect! In Scripture, He healed in different ways but the result was always the same.

Need a miracle today? Don't expect Him to do it in ways He has done before. He will break out of every box we put Him in!

14th November

'A door of effective ministry has opened to me, but there are many who oppose me.' (1 Cor. 16:9)

When a door of **opportunity** opens, the window of **opposition** is never far away!

15th November

'The tempter came to him and said, 'If you are the Son of God, tell these stones to become bread."' (Matt. 4:3)

The battle for Jesus wasn't about food; it was about identity. The enemy wasn't just tempting Jesus to eat; he was tempting Jesus to question...question the most important thing of all - His relationship with the Father.

Wear the helmet of salvation and the breastplate of righteousness. Be totally convinced in your head and in your heart who you are because of whose you are!

16th November

'And he lived in the wilderness until he appeared publicly to Israel.' (Lk. 1:80)

Before John could undertake his public proclamation he needed a private preparation. In order to prepare the way for the Lord he, himself, needed to be prepared by the Lord.

Before any work can be done through you, a work has to be done in you. The wilderness that both Paul (Gal. 1:15ff) and Christ (Matt. 4:1ff) had to experience before their ministries began could never be a fast-track to greatness. Interestingly, for John, his private moulding far outweighed his public ministry - many years 'lost' in the desert yet only six months in the 'limelight'.

Take heart - it's not always quantity of service that counts but quality of service.

However long your race, run it well!

17th November

'Men of Israel, listen to this...' (Acts 2:22)

On the Day of Pentecost, when there was a new experience of the Spirit with strange manifestations, Peter helped his hearers to understand the present happenings by reminding them of their past history.

History can never be repeated exactly, but because the Lord often moves in cycles, if we are to negotiate where we are going, we have to embrace where we have come from. To understand the new shoots we have to remember the older roots.

History is not to be fixated on, but neither should it be forsaken. We ignore the past at our own peril.

18th November

HIS DELAYS ARE NOT HIS DENIALS!

'When Jesus heard that Lazarus was sick, he stayed where he was...' (Jn. 11:6)

It is a fact that God's ways are not our ways. He always seems to have something bigger in store than we can hope or imagine. Mary and Martha were concerned about their brother and they made a reasonable request - 'Lord come, the one you love is sick.' But Jesus didn't come straight away, He delayed and Lazarus died. Martha was bewildered and exclaimed with a hint of blame in her voice, 'If you had been here my brother wouldn't have died.' However, we know the end of the story - Jesus raised Lazarus from the dead after four days.

Many times we make requests of the Lord and He seems 'slow' in answering and acting. We become bewildered and disappointed because He does respond as soon as we ask. In our 'now' generation with our desire for instant results, we become impatient and often take matters into our own hands. We then make things worse and then blame God.

Take heart today, He has heard you and He is very much aware of your need. Though He seems to delay, He does not **deny!** You may have a 'healing' in mind, He has a 'resurrection' in store!

19th November

'And God is able to bless you abundantly, so that in all things at all times, having all that you need, you will abound in every good work.' (2 Cor. 9:8)

Even this day, may you know heavenly provision for your earthly vision!

20th November

'But...at midnight, Paul and Silas were singing hymns and the other prisoners were listening to them...' (Acts 16:25)

There are two occasions when we should praise God - when we feel like it and when we don't. If Paul could sing in a prison, if Jehoshaphat could lift his voice in the face of an enemy he could never naturally defeat (2 Chron. 20:18), if Habakkuk could rejoice though it was all falling apart (Hab. 3:17-18), surely we can too. True worship starts with a decision to praise him in the dark not in the light.

To **rejoice** is a **choice**! Like Paul and Silas, not only is the Lord listening, the world is listening too!

21st November

'Moses my servant is dead.' (Josh. 1:2)

The Lord raises up specific leaders and ministries to suit certain settings. For the Children of Israel, to leave Egypt and journey through the wilderness required someone with shepherding skills - Moses. However, to fight battles and possess the Promised Land needed a military leader - Joshua. One was commissioned to take the people **out**, the other to take the people **in**.

A 'Joshua' trying to shepherd sheep and a 'Moses' trying to strategise soldiers will never work.

Be the type of leader and servant that God has already designed you to be - know your season and be at peace with your limitations.

22nd November

'He determines the number of the stars and calls them each by name.' (Ps. 147:4)

Cosmologists tell us that there are roughly 10 billion galaxies in our universe and each galaxy contains a trillion stars. Just think, that's 10 billion trillion stars that God has both created and counted.

However, according to this verse, if taken literally - these stars move from being **numbered** to being **named**. When you name something it then becomes personally known to you.

Today, even in a world of some 7 billion inhabitants, you are known to the Star Maker by name.

'I have redeemed you, I have called you by name' (Is. 43:1).

Feel special? You should!

23rd November

"Were not all ten healed? Where are the other nine?" (Lk. 17:17)

Why did only one take the time to thank Jesus for their healing? Perhaps the other 90% were so eager to return to normality that they overlooked the One who touched them supernaturally.

Let's not be so caught up with the healing that we forget to thank the Healer, the blessing that we forget the Benefactor or the provision that we forget the Provider.

Miracles in our lives are 'signs' and are never designed to be worshipped. They merely point to the Miracle-worker who is to be worshipped.

Be the 1 in 10.

24th November

'I have learned the secret of being content in any and every situation...' (Phil. 4:12)

On 'Black Friday' when bargains galore are there to be had and as the Western World turns its attention to Christmas shopping with the latest 'must have' items - strive for heavenly contentment instead of earthly commercialism.

True 'contentment' is quite different to 'happiness'. The latter is dependent on positive happenings whereas the former is present even without them.

True contentment is never achieved by striving for more but by being satisfied with what we have. There will always be those who have far more than us but equally there are those on the planet who have far less. How easy it is to spend money we don't have on things we don't need to impress people we don't know.

However, it is worth noting in our 'last minute dot com world' that true contentment is never achieved instantaneously but as Paul himself discovered, it needs to be learned over time.

25th November

'I answered them by saying, 'The God of heaven will give us success." (Neh. 2:20)

The first secret of Nehemiah's success is **Observation**! Whilst surveying the city on his mount one night, he didn't see Jerusalem as it was, he saw it as it could be with faith and hard work - the potential not the present, the possibilities not the problem, a perfect wall, not a pile of stones.

Don't see things as they are, see things as they could be. If you don't see it, you won't see it!

26th November

'I answered them by saying, 'The God of heaven will give us success." (Neh. 2:20)

The second secret of Nehemiah's success is perseverance through **Opposition**! Whenever there are possibilities there are problems. Whenever the Lord opens a door of opportunity, the enemy opens a door of opposition. The wheat and the weeds do seem to grow together and the Early Church prospered in the midst of persecution. The discouraging Sanballat's and Tobiah's that Nehemiah experienced are still alive and kicking today in their various forms. The question is are we going to listen to the critics or to Christ? Are we going to down our tools or up our game?

Today, are you knowing opposition in your own context because of your stand for Christ? Keep going! Keep putting another brick on the wall.

27th November

'I answered them by saying, 'The God of heaven will give us suc-

cess." (Neh. 2:20)

The third secret of Nehemiah's success is **Impartation**! In 2:12 we are told that 'God put something in Nehemiah's heart to do for Jerusalem'. When you have divine impartation, you will give up a good job working for the king to work for the King. When you have divine impartation, you will travel hundreds of miles to build a wall from a pile of rubble. When you have divine impartation, you will keep going in the face of severe opposition.

28th November

'Get yourself ready...Go and proclaim...' (Jer. 1:17, 2:1)

Before the Prophet could **proclaim**, he had to **prepare.**

Getting ready comes before getting going!

29th November

'Deliver me O Lord from a deceitful tongue...' (Ps. 120:2)

The Oxford Dictionary definition of political 'spin' is to 'emphasise certain facts or show bias in certain areas in order to gain favour.' Spin verges on deception.

One of the original 'Kings of Spin' was Jacob, who lived up to the meaning of his name 'Deceiver' with numerous attempts at manipulation, even from birth, and strategic positioning throughout his life to gain both the birthright and blessing - even from kin.

The true Church of Jesus Christ should be the most transparent and trustworthy group of people on the planet. What do we have to hide? Though the secular world may try 'spin' to achieve its goal, for the spiritual man or woman there's simply no place for half-truths and misleading information to gain prominence and position.

Spin is sin...and the wages of spin is death!

30th November

'Then Nathanael declared, 'You are the Son of God!'' (Jn 1:49)

'Then Thomas said, 'My Lord and my God!'' (Jn 20:28)

Interestingly, the Fourth Gospel both begins and ends with a sceptic receiving spiritual insight.

Many things can come from natural information, but certain truth can only come from supernatural revelation.

DECEMBER

1st December

In the community and the Church, there is often much talk about personal and corporate vision but sadly little about personal and corporate values. I've heard of many a 'Vision Sunday' but not a single 'Values Sunday'. Vision needs values and values need vision! Vision is the endgame but values help with the endurance. Vision is about belief but values is about behaviour. As a church or organisation it is not the final result that's important but the relationship with others on the way is imperative. As Christ-followers we can be caught up with the gifts of the Spirit but not the fruit of the Spirit. 1 Corinthians 13 is still between chapters 12 and 14 in my Bible. Both the charismata and character are needed.

A new and extremely challenging year is around the corner and although the 1st January will be no different to the 31st December, we can choose now how the future can be framed for both our personal lives and the organisations we are part of.

It isn't only what we aim for but our attitude on the journey!

2nd December

'The stone the builders rejected has become the cornerstone...' (1 Pet. 2:7)

That which life rejects, the Lord receives and finds resourceful. God did it then, He can do it now!

3rd December

'The Lord will fight for you...you are only to be still...' (Ex. 14:14)

At those times in our lives when we feel trapped and our backs are up against the wall, with the armies of Egypt behind us, the mountains either side and the Red Sea in front - we are merely to let go and let God! On such occasions, we are not to be part of the miracle, mere pointers to the Miracle-worker.

He is still in the business of parting our 'Red Seas', of making a way where, according to both public and private perception, there seems to be no way. Don't just face it, faith it!

4th December

"How long, O Lord, must I call for help...?" (Hab. 1:2)

"Yet will I rejoice in the Lord" (Hab. 3:18)

The book of Habakkuk is a series of complaints to the Almighty from a mere mortal - an argument with God over His unfathomable and seemingly unjust ways. In reply to his concerns, the Lord did answer - all will come good in the end. The man of God needed to rest in God's appointments and not be destroyed by life's many disappointments. The end of the book sees a private complaint becoming a public confession - of praise!

Though we may complain at both the world around us and our own world - the macro and the micro - may our inner complaints become outward confessions of the One who does work all things together for good for those who love Him.

5th December

'Some men came, bringing to him a paralyzed man...' (Mk 2:3)

True friendship isn't just about praying for others but being practical with others. In a crisis don't just grab hold of God, grab a corner of someone's mat. Sometimes our holy hands have to get dirty to see breakthroughs in others people's circumstances. Remember, on this occasion it was the faith of the faithful few that brought about the healing of their friend.

6th December

'I, being in the way, the Lord led me...' (Gen. 24:27)

Guidance for the Christ-follower should not be a series of stop/start motions but a smooth synergy - being in a vibrant and on-going relationship with our Guide who not only knows the way, but is the Way.

It's always easier to steer a moving vehicle!

7th December

'My ears had heard of you but now my eyes have seen you.' (Job 42:5)

May we not only hear about the Lord, may we go on to see Him!

Hearing produces **information**, seeing comes from **revelation!**

8th December

"Father, not my will, but yours be done" (Mk 14:36)

I hear, yet again, of another believer who has chosen to take an unbiblical path for their life. No doubt they have known a battle of conscience but now feel they should 'follow their heart' and 'be true to themselves' - such statements may be popular in the world right now but find no justification in the Word.

In Gethsemane, after a battle of wills, I'm so glad that the Saviour of the World chose the will of the Father not the way of the flesh. The latter may have meant instant peace for Him, but it would have caused an everlasting problem for you and me. Our eternal salvation rests on those words, 'Not my will, but yours be done.'

The cross continues to be a symbol of death, not for Christ any longer but now for the Christ-follower, death to what we want and this still remains the very essence of daily discipleship.

Don't follow your own heart, which remains deceitful, but follow God's heart as revealed in His Word. Be true to Scripture not self. Not my will, Lord, but yours be done!

9th December

Hebrews 9:24-28

The 3 stages of the ministry of Christ:

- He **has** appeared (v26) - His Incarnation (In the Past)

- He **is** appearing (v24) – His High Priestly role (In the Present)

- He **will** appear (v28) - His Second Coming (In the Future)

Christ has been active, He is active and He will be active!

10th December

"You will give him the name 'Jesus' for he will save his people from their sins" (Matt. 1:21)

Jesus was born in order to one day die. One of the gifts given to the Christ-child (Matt. 2:11) - later at the cross and the crypt - was myrrh, a natural painkiller (Mk 15:23) and a resin used to embalm dead bodies (Jn 19:39). In many ways myrrh was a symbol of suffering and death - symbolic of what was to come for the young Saviour.

You can't separate Christmas from Calvary! The cradle is closely followed by the cross and the crypt.

11th December

AWAY WITH THE MANGER?

'It's a Wonderful Life!' is a Christmas classic and ranked by the American Film Institute as 'the most inspirational film of all time'. It tells the story of George Bailey who thinks that his life has not amounted to anything and so considers ending it all on a snowy Christmas Eve by jumping from a bridge. An angel called Clarence rescues him and shows George how different the world, his home and his community would have been had he never been born. The revelation transforms him!

What if Jesus had never been born? What if there was no nativity, no manger, no star in the East. The mere idea is unthinkable!

- We would not know what God was like (Jn 14:9);
- We would not know forgiveness of sins (1 Tim. 1:15);
- We would not have eternal life (Jn 3:16);
- The devil's works would not have been destroyed (1 Jn 3:8);
- The world would be in darkness (Jn 12:46).

This Christmas, thank God for Jesus!

12th December

'He called together the teachers of the law and asked where the Messiah was to be born. 'In Bethlehem in Judea,' they replied' (Matt. 2:4-5)

It is interesting that the 'experts' knew correctly where the Promised One was to be born, yet they did not go themselves to see Him. How easy to know the details of Scripture in our heads yet be unmoved in our hearts to act upon them. How easy to direct others, yet stay put ourselves.

The Word of God should always lead us to the worship of God!

13th December

"Glory to God in the highest, and on earth peace to men..." (Lk. 2:14)

Notice the order declared by the angel - it's 'Glory to God' first and then 'peace amongst men' will follow. World peace won't lead to the glorification of God because it can never truly happen outside of the 'Prince of Peace.' Only when God is truly acknowledged and appreciated through His Son, will local and global peace take place. Vertical then horizontal!

14th December

O LITTLE TOWN OF BETHLEHEM

'She wrapped him in cloths and placed him in a manger...' (Lk. 2:7)

How interesting that the Saviour of the World was born in Bethlehem. A passage in the Mishnah leads to the conclusion that the lambs which pastured on the nearby hills were destined for temple sacrifice in Jerusalem at Passover time.

The Passover lambs were kept by specially trained and purified shepherds. The lambs were born in the 'tower of the flock' known as Migdal Eder under the watchful eye of the shepherds who would then inspect them for imperfections and either certify them for use as sacrifices in the temple or designate them to be released for common use. The new, spotless lambs would, according to some sources, even be wrapped in special swaddling clothes once certified.

Thirty years after the birth of Christ, John the Baptist saw him and declared, 'Behold, the Lamb of God, who takes away the sin of the world!' (Jn 1:29). The One born at Bethlehem was to be sacrificed in Jerusalem.

Christmas and Calvary come together!

15th December

'Now there was a man in Jerusalem called Simeon...It had been revealed to him by the Holy Spirit that he would not die before he had seen the Lord's Messiah.' (Lk. 2:25-26)

Waiting to see the fulfilment of what God has promised is difficult whether the waiting period is days, weeks, months or even years. In our instant world we tend to lose patience and fill in the gap between the initial revelation and final reception with worry, wondering and even working the details out ourselves. But there is always a gestation period in God's plan and preparation - a time to grow in excitement and exhilaration. Our waiting times should become worship times! When we finally see the promise fulfilled and take it in our arms - it will be worth it all.

Before the fulfilment, be faithful!

16th December

If you see the word 'XMAS' at this time of year don't despair- it doesn't necessarily mean that Christ is being left out of His own birthday celebrations.

X is the Greek letter 'Ch' - the first two letters of 'Christ'.

Early believers, in the midst of severe persecution between 64 and 313AD, when meeting strangers would write an X for both speed and subtlety to indicate to other Christians they were disciples of Christ. One would draw a diagonal line and the other would draw another to intersect it and the X would be formed. Alternatively, one would draw an arch and the other would draw another one underneath until a fish symbol could be seen. Fellowship could then start between the two. Such symbols and secret signs were not obvious to their oppressors.

17th December

'He emptied himself...took on the nature of a servant and was found in human likeness....he humbled himself to death on a cross...' (Phil. 2:7-8)

When God became man it wasn't what He gave up that requires

our attention, but more so what He took on that calls for our adoration. It's not what He left behind in Heaven, but what He became on Earth. He took on **flesh** so He could then take our **failures**, human **skin** to take our **sin**.

The Crib and the Cross come together!

18th December

'All of us have sinned and fallen short of God's saving presence.' (Rom. 3:23)

If God was Santa Claus, we would all be on the 'Naughty List' - everyone without exception.

Both Mother Teresa and Billy Graham were once asked if getting into Heaven was by doing good works, on a scale of 1-10, where would they stand. Mother Teresa said '7' and Dr Graham said '5'. In comparison to these great 'saints' of old, I don't stand a chance!

However, the good news of Christmas and, in fact, every day, is that God knew I could never make the 'Nice List' on my own. He sent His only Son, born of a virgin, born in a stable, to be my Saviour. This same Jesus, didn't stay in the manger, but grew up in every way that we grow - physically, mentally, socially and spiritually. However, different to us, He never did anything wrong. Never an incorrect thought, word or action in 33 years on earth. He was the perfect child, the perfect teenager, the perfect adult. Because of this important fact He was able to be a worthy sacrifice before a Holy God and to take my place on the Cross. He took my 'naughtiness' and now declares me 'nice!'

I may not be on Santa's 'Nice List' this year - I hope I am. I hope he checks it twice! However, more importantly, I am in the Lamb's Book of Life and my name is recorded in indelible ink. Not because of my works, but because of His work from the Crib to Calvary.

19th December

"Today in the town of David a Saviour has been born to you; he is Christ, the Lord" (Lk. 2:11)

Not only is He the Saviour of our sins, but He should be the Lord of our lives. Not only did He carry a cross, He now wears a crown

- He's Saviour and Sovereign!

20th December

'Jesus said, 'I am the bread of life: he that comes to me shall never hunger." (Jn 6:35)

Interestingly, the name 'Bethlehem' in Hebrew means, 'the house of bread'. Although the Christ had to be born in this insignificant city in order to fulfil Micah's prophecy some 700 years before in order to validate His position and person, on a practical level today, it is no accident that the Bread of Life was born in the Place of Bread.

Natural bread can satisfy a natural hunger, but for a short while. We then become hungry again and crave physical fulfilment once more. As with the physical, so with the spiritual. It is easy to get caught up in searching for meaning in life from the wrong things because there are many things that bring a temporary fix and moments of happiness. But only Christ satisfies the eternal dimension of the human spirit long-term. Anything, or anyone else, may satisfy the spirit - but just for a short while.

Don't eat from the wrong table. The Bread of Life from the Place of Bread offers this for free. Like any gift, this can't be earned but must be accepted.

21st December

'An angel appeared and said, 'take the child and escape to Egypt for Herod is going to search for the child, to kill him." (Matt. 2:13)

The young Messiah, together with His parents, were arguably the first refugees found in the New Testament. They were displaced, forced to cross national boundaries and were those who could not return home safely due to death threats.

These days we don't need to board a boat nor cross a continent to find refugees. They are all around us. Think of them this Christmas, seek them out on your road or in your town and do what you can. They are closer than we realise. We can't change everyone's world everywhere, but we can change somebody's world somewhere.

22nd December

A STAR AND THE SPIRIT

'He will not speak of himself but he will glorify me.' (Jn 16:13)

At some point after that first Christmas, a star in the sky directed the wise men to Jesus and having discovered Him, they were soon led to worship Him - later their steps taking a different path. However, this 'Christmas star' soon fulfilled its purpose of guiding, gladdening and guarding and was gone.

Today, we are not left without a guide. Although a temporary star no longer points to Christ, His Spirit has been sent from heaven and permanently leads us to meet, glorify and worship not a Child but a crucified and risen Conqueror!

Wise men seek Him still!

23rd December

God came down at Christmas to:

- **SAVE** us (Matt. 1:21)
- **SHOW** us (Jn 14:9)
- **SYMPATHISE** with us (Heb. 4:15)

Truly Immanuel - God with us! At Christmas, He took on skin - at Easter, He took our sin!

24th December

'When the time was right, God sent his Son....' (Gal. 4:4)

Ever thought why Jesus was sent when He was? Why not earlier or later? The Father sent the Son at a very strategic time in world history. Various forces were shaping the then known world including the political force of Rome, the cultural force of Greece and the religious force of Judaism that had dispersed around the world some 500 years previously. Interestingly, the Lord used such shaping forces to prepare mankind's hearts and aid the spread of the Gospel - the Roman Peace, ease of travel, the ability to preach in a universal language without the need for translation and the awareness of One God through the Jewish diaspora. Within thirty years after Christ's resurrection, the Christians had 'turned the world upside down' or, in fact, the right way up! Caesar wasn't in charge but Christ was.

God still has a strategy, not only for His world but for your world. He is in the detail and is never too early or too late but always on time. Trust his timing today!

25th December

'And he will be called 'Immanuel' which means, 'God is with us'' (Matt.1:23)

God's present to mankind was His presence! No longer a sense of 'God is nowhere' but the security of knowing that 'God is now here!'

26th December

'If anyone desires to come after me, let him deny himself, and take up his cross and follow me...' (Lk. 9:23)

Today is St Stephen's Day! As we remember the first Christian martyr, forget not the estimated 100,000+ lives that were laid down this past year around the world for the cause of Christ. The ultimate persecution is not only a mark of true discipleship (Matt. 16:24ff) but is a sign of Christ's Return (Matt. 24:9). Until then, the martyrs' blood continues to be 'the seed of the Church.'

27th December

'The Lord will give that which is good...' (Ps. 85:12)

God does not give His children what they perceive to be good but what He, Himself, knows to be genuinely good. Not receiving what you're requesting? Perhaps it's not right for you.

Outward appearances can still be deceiving. All that glitters is not always gold!

28th December

'Grow in the grace and knowledge of the Lord Jesus Christ' (2 Pet. 3:18)

Before starting comprehensive school at the age of 11, I remember going out one morning to buy my school uniform with my mother. What sticks out in my mind most of all was trying on a blazer that was clearly too big for me at that particular time in my life. After querying the size I still remember the answer that came back, 'You're going through a growth spurt - You'll grow into it before you know.' Sure enough, I did. Mother knows best!

Maybe the task that God has revealed to you doesn't seem to fit and appears too large at this moment in time. Perhaps your current knowledge of Christ is not as full as you feel it should be. Take heart - You'll grow into it! Look not at your current predicament but future possibilities and dress for where you're going not for where you are. Father knows best!

May this coming year be one when you experience a spiritual growth spurt.

29th December

'Then Samuel placed a stone at Mizpah exclaiming, 'Thus far, the Lord has helped us!'' (1 Sam. 7:12)

Looking back at the past year, though there may have been battles amongst the blessings, riots in addition to revivals and opposition amidst the opportunities, what memorials of God's goodness can you raise today?

I'm certain that if we stop to count our blessings, to name them one by one, it will truly surprise us what the Lord has done!

30th December

LET IT GO!

'And forgive us our debts, as we also have forgiven our debt-

ors.' (Matt. 6:12)

There are various words for 'forgive' in the original biblical languages. In this famous passage, it literally means 'to release' or 'to leave' and is used again by the despondent disciple in Matt. 19:27, 'We have **left** everything to follow you'. True forgiveness is not a feeling but a choice - a choice to leave and let go. Three important and practical points about forgiveness:

Forgiveness is not trying to forget, but the opposite - it's actually remembering without resentment;

Although you forgive a person it doesn't mean you still trust that person. Forgiveness takes you back to a foundation where trust needs to build again;

Forgiveness shown by God to us and forgiveness we show to others is usually linked together in Scripture. He has set the standard - we show because He has shown and continues to show.

Been hurt? Been offended? Been let down? Been betrayed? A servant is not above his master. You are in good company with Christ who chose forgiveness on the cross. Choose now to let it go, let that person go and set yourself free in the process.

31st December

'Forgetting what is behind and straining toward what is ahead, I press on toward the goal to win the prize for which God has called me heavenward in Christ Jesus.' (Phil. 3:13-14)

Here the Apostle Paul is once again using the analogy of a race. The most successful athletes forget the problems of past laps and obstacles and fix their eyes on the future podium and prize - running towards it with every fibre of their being.

Perhaps you've hit a few hurdles this past year and have stumbled off course. Perhaps you're not as far on as you thought you would be and seem to have been overtaken by others. Take heart, you're still in the race and it's never how you start but whether you finish. Run your own race in the lane He has marked out for you looking to the One who is still cheering you on. Learn from the past but don't live in the past. Obstacles are there to overcome - not to stop you but to spur you on.

Remember, you can only be an overcomer if you've had something to overcome.

Printed in Great Britain
by Amazon

75515106R00092